TOP YOUTUBE STARS

LINDSEY STIRLING

Violinist with More than 2 BILLION VIEWS

HENRIETTA TOTH

rosen publishing's
rosen central®

New York

For my niece Emi, who has taught me a lot about YouTube

Published in 2020 by The Rosen Publishing Group, Inc.
29 East 21st Street, New York, NY 10010

First Edition

Library of Congress Cataloging-in-Publication Data

Names: Toth, Henrietta, author.
Title: Lindsey Stirling: Violinist with More than 2 Billion Views / Henrietta Toth.
Description: New York : Rosen Publishing Group, 2020. | Series: Top YouTube stars | Includes bibliographical references and index.
Identifiers: LCCN 2018054344 | ISBN 9781725346284 (library bound) | ISBN 9781725346277 (pbk.)
Subjects: LCSH: Stirling, Lindsey, 1986– —Juvenile literature. | Violinists—United States—Biography—Juvenile literature. | Composers—United States—Biography—Juvenile literature. | LCGFT: Biographies.
Classification: LCC ML3930.S76 T67 2020 | DDC 787.2092 [B]—dc23
LC record available at https://lccn.loc.gov/2018054344

Manufactured in the United States of America

On the cover: Dancer, violinist, and YouTube phenomenon Lindsey Stirling attends the 2015 AOL BUILD Speaker Series in New York City.

CONTENTS

Doing two things at the same time is not an easy task. It is, however, a talent and a skill that has made American violinist and dancer Lindsey Stirling a top YouTube star. Stirling loves to play the violin and she loves to dance. So she combined her love of both into an unusual performance style as a dancing violinist.

At the beginning of her career, Stirling was not sure if a dancing violinist could be successful. While she was in college, Stirling tried playing her violin to hip-hop tracks as she danced. She performed at small clubs, parties, talent shows, and every open-mic night she could find. She knew she might be on the right career track when she played at a carnival-like neighborhood block party and saw herself billed as a hip-hop violinist.

Putting a modern twist on traditional violin playing earned Stirling the distinction of being the highest-paid female YouTube star in 2015. *Forbes* magazine listed Stirling among its 30 Under 30 in Music: The Class of 2015. During her rise to stardom, Stirling has stayed true to her unique artistic vision despite criticism from music critics. She told Samantha Sharf of *Forbes*, "The reason I succeeded is the exact reason I was told I would never succeed. I was different."

Stirling plays cover songs and also writes her own music and songs and has recorded four albums. She won a Billboard Music Award for her albums *Shatter Me* in 2015 and in 2017 for *Brave Enough*. Stirling tours the world performing in concerts and collaborates with well-known artists. She has also become a best-selling author. *The Only Pirate at the Party* is an autobiography of her childhood and her path to success. The book made the *New York Times* bestseller list in 2016. As a philanthropist, Stirling worked with the Atlanta Music Project to raise money for young people

Lindsey Stirling gives an energetic performance in Orange County, California, on April 2, 2013.

to learn about music and to perform in orchestras. In 2014, Stirling performed with Cirque du Soleil to celebrate World Water Day and to encourage water conservation.

Stirling knows that many factors have helped her become successful and also to overcome challenges. For many years, she battled the eating disorder anorexia nervosa. She has also had to cope with the illnesses and deaths of her longtime band member and friend, Jason Gaviati, and then her father, Stephen J. Stirling. Her religious faith as a member of the Church of Jesus Christ of Latter-Day Saints and the people who have come into her life have helped Stirling work through her career and personal problems. However, Stirling credits YouTube for giving her a platform for her musical performance when no one else was interested. YouTube also allowed Stirling the freedom to present her music her way. "I stumbled upon YouTube because I didn't know what else to do, and it's the best thing that ever happened to me," she told Nick Krewen of the *Toronto Star*.

CHAPTER ONE

A Humble Childhood

To learn to dance or to play the violin? That was the question in Lindsey Stirling's humble childhood. Growing up in a modest home, Stirling had to choose between two things she wanted to do. Yet, Stirling values her upbringing since it helped her to develop her artistic creativity. She made toys out of cardboard boxes and costumes from old clothes. These early skills would one day come in handy on her way to YouTube success.

Lindsey Stirling poses with her sister Brooke S. Passey at the AOL Build Speaker Series in New York City on January 12, 2016.

THE EARLY YEARS

Lindsey Stirling was born in Santa Ana, California, on September 21, 1986, to Stephen and Diane Stirling. She had an older sister named Jennifer, and two years later her younger sister Brooke was born. Lindsey also has two siblings, Marina and Vladimir, whom her parents adopted from Russia when she was in college. Lindsey was eight years old when her family moved to Gilbert, Arizona, where she grew up.

SURROUNDED BY MUSIC

Music has been a large part of Stirling's life from a very young age. Her parents liked classical music and played records at home. They also took Stirling and her siblings to concerts. "I can remember dancing around the living room with my two sisters to the music of Paganini and Mozart. I can still remember my dad combing the newspaper circling all the free concerts in town and on the weekends, we would go as a family," she recalled to Erik Kain of *Forbes*.

Stirling's desire to play violin came from watching the orchestras perform. She explained to Laurie Niles of Violinist.com, "Being exposed to so much classical music, I realized that the violin is the star of the orchestra. Today, kids see MTV—they see Taylor Swift and Katy Perry, and they want to be them. But I was exposed to violin music, and seeing that the violins have the solos, I thought, 'That's the star!'"

A DIFFICULT CHOICE

At age five, Stirling begged her parents for violin lessons. She also wanted to learn how to dance. "Ever since I was a kid, I've always wished that I could dance, but my parents said, 'You can choose violin or you can choose dance, but we can't afford both,' and I chose violin," she said in an interview with NewMediaRockstars.com. Today, dancing in her videos has fulfilled her childhood wish.

Stirling started learning to play the violin at age six using the Suzuki method of instruction. Her parents could afford only half lessons, but it was difficult to find a teacher who would give just fifteen-minute lessons once a week. Stirling practiced every day on secondhand, rented violins until she got her own instrument in the sixth grade.

SOME THINGS TO KNOW ABOUT STIRLING

Her Favorite Food Is Cereal

Stirling loves to eat cereal and has fond memories of sitting on the living room floor eating a bowl of cereal with her father.

She Loves All Things Disney

Stirling loves Disneyland and Disney characters and sometimes wishes she could live in a Disney movie. A bit of that wish came true when she competed on "Disney Night" on *Dancing with the Stars*. She danced the foxtrot to the song "When You Wish Upon a Star" from the Disney movie *Pinocchio*.

Her Favorite Television Show Is *Project Runway*

Stirling loves fashion and costume design. She pieced together odd bits of clothing and material to design the costumes for her early videos.

THE PIRATE LOOK

In the second grade, Stirling had poor reading skills. She was smart in other areas and talented on her violin, but she found reading difficult. Stirling was diagnosed with cross-dominance. It is a learning disability marked by language and scholastic difficulties and mental health issues. It means that Stirling's brain processed what she saw differently. Stirling writes in her autobiography, *The Only Pirate at the Party*, that for her cross-dominance was "a lot like dyslexia, only completely different."

The treatment included wearing an eye patch over her right eye. Stirling did not like wearing the eye patch until she imagined

Coauthor Brooke S. Passey looks on as Lindsey Stirling, with her dog, Luna, speaks during a book signing for *The Only Pirate at the Party* in Austin, Texas, on January 16, 2016.

she looked like a pirate and became interested in how pirates lived. "Pirates don't take orders or ask permission," Stirling writes in her book. "They do what they want. Allow me to clarify. If your mom asks you to do the dishes, do not pull out your pirate attitude. But if someone tells you you're not good enough, says your dreams are too lofty, or claims there is no room in showbiz for a dancing violinist—well then, by all means, pull out your eye patch, my friend, and take to the high seas."

RETHINKING THE VIOLIN

By her late teens, Stirling lost her enthusiasm for playing the violin. The strict method of instruction did not leave room for Stirling to add her personal interpretation to the classical pieces she was learning. But by playing music she was interested in listening to, such as pop tunes, Stirling learned to love the violin again. While attending Mesquite High School in Gilbert, Arizona, Stirling was in a rock band called Stomp on Melvin. She began to write her own music and develop her unique dance performance. Stirling explained to Laurie Niles of Violinist.com, "Rather than giving up on it when I started to get burned out, and I wanted to be more creative with it, to be able to create art and not just play what other people had created. So rather than switching instruments or giving up on what I had worked so hard to do, I just thought, no, I need to make the violin fit me, rather than make me fit the violin."

CHAPTER TWO

A Dancing Violinist

"Be yourself; everyone else is already taken." Stirling begins her autobiography, *The Only Pirate at the Party*, with this line from writer Oscar Wilde. Stirling realized early on that she did not have to be like everyone else to be accepted. She knew she should love herself as she was and with the talent she had.

"YOU'RE TOO DIFFERENT"

Everywhere Stirling performed she was told, "You're too different." Stirling told Morgan Jones of *Deseret News*, "I was told at first that being different was a bad thing. Everywhere I went, it was just, 'You're too different.' And it turned out that being different was the best thing that ever happened to my career. It is why people travel to my shows. It's why people want to hear my story and buy my book. The recipe for my success is that I stayed true to that." Stirling does not fit the usual stereotype of a violinist or a dancer but being different is okay with her. It has helped Stirling learn not to be bothered by criticism and rejection and still work hard.

Stirling was inspired to combine dance with violin playing by groups like Celtic Woman and Bond. Her performances were a little disorderly at first until all the parts fell into place to create her own presentation. Stirling always believed that she could succeed if she got the right breaks. She just didn't dream that it could be on such a large scale.

BEFORE YOUTUBE

Stirling's musical style started to come together when she performed during America's Junior Miss Pageant (now Distinguished Young Women Award) in 2005. She won the talent category in the state pageant with her performance of a violin rock song she wrote.

Lindsey Stirling plays her violin during the SXSW (South by Southwest) Music Festival at the Austin Music Hall in Austin, Texas, on March 15, 2014.

To launch her career, Stirling performed wherever she could get noticed. She played small gigs, like bar mitzvahs and weddings. She even played for free at some music events. When Stirling performed at a large block party, she was billed, for the first time, as a hip-hop violinist. Stirling tried to get talent agents, television shows, and record producers interested in her music but was not successful.

America's Got Talent's panel of judges, Piers Morgan (*left*), Sharon Osbourne (*second from right*), and Howie Mandel (*right*), appear along with host Nick Cannon to speak with reporters on April 15, 2011, in Pasadena, California.

ON *AMERICA'S GOT TALENT*

In 2010, Stirling was a contestant on the fifth season of the reality television show *America's Got Talent*. She was introduced as a hip-hop violinist, and she played and danced to "Tik Tok" by Kesha and "Break Your Heart" by Taio Cruz.

Seven million viewers tuned in to watch Stirling reach the quarterfinals. For Stirling, it was a moment of success. She won the audience's approval, but her performance did not sway the judges. They liked her interesting presentation yet they were not impressed by her musical skills. Judge Piers Morgan told Stirling, "You're not untalented, but you're not good enough to get away with flying through the air and trying to play the violin at the same time." Judge Sharon Osbourne said, "You need to be in a group. What you're doing is not enough to fill a theater in Vegas."

AFTER *AMERICA'S GOT TALENT*

Stirling had hoped that because *America's Got Talent* had a large audience, it would boost her career and change her life. She admitted that it was not her best performance, but she had given it her best shot. Stirling was hurt and humiliated by the judges' comments and disappointed in the show's results. "After that, the world had completely forgotten that I had existed and I went back to square zero. I kept hustling for six months and doing things like getting really low-key gigs at college campuses,

HOW TO LAUNCH A YOUTUBE CHANNEL

The popularity and influence of YouTube continues to grow. Thirty million people across the world check daily to see what's new on You-Tube. Videos can be easily filmed on a smartphone, edited on a laptop, and then uploaded to your channel.

It's simple to follow the directions on the YouTube website to start a channel. First, determine who your audience will be. For whom will you be making videos? Look at the competition and see what you can do differently. Then, produce your first video and create your channel. Give your video a title that can be easily searched on Google. Finally, set up a schedule to produce new videos and film at least one each week.

playing at noon in cafeterias," she told Nick Krewen of the *Toronto Star*. Although Stirling kept dancing and playing her violin, she also thought about quitting.

STIRLING'S FIRST VIDEO

In 2011, when Stirling's career seemed to be fizzling out, she was asked to shoot a music video by videographer Devin Graham. He produces adventure and sports videos for his YouTube channel devinsupertramp. As of early 2019, he has more than 5.3 million subscribers and more than 1 billion views.

Graham told Stirling that he thought she was talented. He wanted to make a music video of her and put it on his YouTube channel. At the time, Stirling didn't know much about YouTube and how it might help her career. Stirling's first music video was filmed against the background of a parking garage and a green park as she played her original song "Spontaneous Me." It was viewed by twenty-five thousand subscribers on Graham's channel. It kicked off Stirling's career as she gathered more views and she began filming videos for her own YouTube channel. Stirling was on her way to YouTube success, and to date, her first video has more than thirty million views.

CHAPTER THREE

YouTube Stardom

A ccording to Stirling, life is about getting one chance after another and recognizing those chances to reach your dreams. In Stirling's case, the chance to produce albums, do concert tours, and work with music stars came in the form of YouTube.

KEY TO SUCCESS

Stirling joined YouTube in 2007. She named her channel Lindseystomp. She had uploaded a video that failed to get her on the *Ellen DeGeneres Show*. It was only after the huge response to making the video of "Spontaneous Me" with Devin Graham that Stirling saw how YouTube could be the platform for her career. "We did the video, 'Spontaneous Me,' and I was amazed. As soon as he put it up on his channel, my music, which was just sitting around on iTunes, suddenly started to sell. People were requesting more of my songs and they were loving and sharing them," Stirling told Nick Krewen of the *Toronto Star*.

In 2012, Stirling posted her breakout song and video "Crystallize" to her own YouTube channel. In it, Stirling plays the violin

Lindsey Stirling takes part in the Forbes Under 30 Summit held at the Pennsylvania Convention Center in Philadelphia on October 5, 2015.

while dancing in a palace made of ice. Within twenty-four hours, the video had one million views. Now it has more than two hundred million views.

AN ONLINE AUDIENCE

Stirling launched a traditional music career in a nontraditional way and found an audience online. In just four years, Stirling went from being unknown to being a star on YouTube and beyond. Millions of fans love her energetic and unique style of performance that includes colorful costumes. Stirling dubsteps and hip-hops her way through a variety of music. She plays her own original songs, cover songs, and her version of video game theme songs like "The Legend of Zelda."

Now, more than eleven million viewers subscribe to Lindsey Stirling (the new name of lindseystomp), making Stirling one of the highest-paid YouTubers. Her videos have been viewed more than two billion times.

The YouTube icon is easily recognized on smartphones and tablets around the world.

MAKING MUSIC VIDEOS

Even though success has happened quickly for Stirling, it has been hard work to launch and maintain her career. She is involved in every aspect of her concerts and videos from the costumes to the dance routines. Stirling makes her own videos for her channel. She learned filmmaking as a student at Brigham Young University, which, in the beginning, helped her to make professional-looking videos on a limited budget. Stirling is particularly good at editing her videos and loves piecing them together.

These days, Stirling makes an income from the ads and sponsors on her channel. Stirling says she is okay with sponsorship

PROS AND CONS OF YOUTUBE

Pros
- YouTube is a reliable platform for uploading content.
- YouTube accepts homemade and professional videos.
- Developing content for YouTube can be done inexpensively.
- YouTube offers a platform for creativity, entertainment, and education.
- YouTube reaches a large audience across the world.
- Some YouTubers make a living through their channels.

Lindsey Stirling performs in a fountain while shooting the music video for "Master of Tides" at the Americana at Brand shopping complex in Glendale, California, on August 14, 2014.

Cons

- **There's pressure to produce and upload content to your channel on a schedule.**
- **Pressure also exists to keep the content fun and interesting for fans.**
- **Being a YouTube celebrity can be tiring, and some YouTubers suffer from burnout.**
- **Fake views of videos can inflate the real number of people watching a channel.**
- **Online safety is a concern, and as a result performers must avoid revealing personal information.**
- **Making a living as a YouTuber is not guaranteed.**

as long as the promotions are not something she or her fans are ashamed of. It allows her to create her music independently.

It's hard for Stirling to choose which is her favorite video. She told the staff of *LDS Living*, "I have creatively put so much personal love and effort into all of my videos that there's a special place in my heart for all of them. I like different videos for different reasons. I think 'Roundtable Rival' is the most fun of all my videos, 'Shatter Me' carries the deepest meaning and is the most personal, and 'Shadows' is classic Lindsey—probably my most innovative creation."

AN INDEPENDENT ARTIST

Since 2012, Stirling has produced four albums. Two went gold and all came in at the top of the classical and dance charts. She has released her albums independently on her own record label Lindseystomp Records. There is no major record company involved. This has given Stirling the artistic freedom to create her music and performances without interference. Thousands of her albums have sold to a growing number of fans enthusiastic about her individual style.

Stirling has been called a classical-crossover violinist, a hip-hop violinist, a pop violinist, and even a New Age musician. But Stirling has her own idea about her style of music. "If I can only choose one category, I'd probably put it in the electronic, because the base of the music is electronic," Stirling explained to George Varga of the *San Diego Union-Tribune*. Stirling sees the violin as the lead performer in her music with the keyboards and synthesizers backing it up.

At the start of her musical career, Stirling thought she had to follow the traditional path and get a talent agent and record contract. Being unable to interest a record company in her music and then finding YouTube was really her big break. Stirling told George Varga of the *San Diego Union-Tribune*, "I just can't believe this journey my music has taken me on. My big goal was that I wanted to be someone who was pioneering the way for the independent artist with this new social media–fueled model, and show that you could cross over from YouTube and be seen as a new artist."

CHAPTER FOUR

Rise to Fame

A s Stirling's online audience grew, she became popular and successful in the United States and abroad, especially in Europe. Companies started to offer Stirling and Devin Graham money to film her videos in exchange for publicity. She explained to Nick Krewen of the *Toronto Star*:

> Once we started to make a name for ourselves, people started to reach out and offer to fly me and Devin places. A travel company paid all our expenses and paid us on top of it to make a video and go to Kenya. The same thing happened in New Zealand. That was the amazing thing— once we were creating such high-quality content, we were able to fund our travels.

CONCERT TOURS

Stirling started doing concert tours in 2012. She has played sold-out events all over the world in large theaters like Humphreys Concerts by the Bay in San Diego, California, that seat 1,400 people. She has been on a two-month tour of North America and played as many as two hundred shows in two years. Sometimes Stirling is on the road for months at a time. She likes traveling with her band on a cozy tour bus and often writes music on those late-night travels from city to city. *Brave Enough*, the name of Stirling's third album and tour, took place in 2016. The tour was filmed as a documentary for the YouTube Red channel. The film looks at how personal challenges and heartbreak affected Stirling's life and concert performance.

Stirling loves to tell a story through her music and stage performance. "I love getting to transform all these songs, all these music videos, into a live performance. It's like a full emotional experience when I create a show," she told John J. Moser of the

Lindsey Stirling takes an athletic leap into the air while performing at the Bass Concert Hall in Austin, Texas, on November 7, 2016.

Morning Call. Stirling wants her audience to go on a journey with her and laugh or cry. She uses video and lighting effects and colorful costumes. Some of Stirling's dancing is athletic, so sneakers are often part of her ensemble. Stirling admits that dancing while playing the violin takes practice. She rehearses a song until she knows it well enough to dance to it.

Stirling has appeared in many different types of shows. She has played at the Kennedy Center in Washington, DC, an NBA game half-time show, and a show held in a large fountain. Stirling plays acoustic and electric violins. Her favorite instrument is an old Roth violin that has a warm sound. Her Yamaha electric violin has a clean and sharp sound. Stirling has taken violin lessons again to brush up on her skills.

STIRLING AND HER CRITICS

Some music critics have been hard on Stirling, especially at the beginning of her career. They did not like her style of performance or her music. They said it lacked boldness, emotion, and sounded like background music. They also did not know whether to label it classical or pop music. More recently, critics have noticed that Stirling has polished her performance, but some still criticize her violin playing. Stirling has been disappointed by the critics' comments, but she admits that she cannot please everyone. She also understands that classically trained violinists might not appreciate her music. But Stirling is having the last laugh because her fans are enthusiastic about her songs, videos, and concerts. They have even told her they like having her music on in the background when they are doing something else.

AWARDS AND RECOGNITION

In 2013, early in her career, Stirling won a YouTube Music Award. She shared the award with the group Pentatonix for its song "Radioactive." Stirling has been nominated for and won Billboard Music Awards. Her debut album, *Lindsey Stirling*, was nominated in 2014. In 2015, she won the Billboard Music Award for Top Dance/ Electronic Album for *Shatter Me*.

Lindsey Stirling and dancer Mark Ballas are pictured at the *Dancing with the Stars* competition in Los Angeles, California, on November 6, 2017.

At the awards ceremony, Stirling and Wiz Khalifa performed a tribute to actor Paul Walker, who died in 2013. Stirling's album *Brave Enough* won Top Dance/ Electronic Album again in 2017.

In 2016, Stirling won Best YouTube Musician at the Shorty Awards, given for the best artist in social media. Her international awards include a win in Germany with an ECHO Award in 2014 for Best Crossover Act. Stirling has appeared and performed at other ceremonies, too, like the MTV Music Awards. However, she still gets uneasy walking those red-carpet events.

WORKING WITH OTHER ARTISTS

Stirling's success has given her the opportunity to collaborate with well-known musical artists. It was a special experience for Stirling to work with the group Evanescence. She had listened to them when she was in high school. Stirling appeared in concert with Andrea Bocelli at the O2 Arena in London. She filmed a video with singer John Legend, in which they perform his song "All of Me." It has more than one hundred million views. Stirling had fun filming a comical video with the Muppets and singer Josh Groban. In it, Kermit the Frog directed Groban and Stirling performing the song "Pure Imagination" from the 1971 movie *Willy Wonka and the Chocolate Factory*.

ON *DANCING WITH THE STARS*

In the fall of 2017, Stirling joined the cast of *Dancing with the Stars* for its twenty-fifth season. Stirling got to express her love of dancing and storytelling through her performances. She was paired with instructor Mark Ballas and presented different dances like the foxtrot, tango, and waltz. During the freestyle dance, Stirling played her electric violin. Stirling placed second at the end of the competition.

CHAPTER FIVE

Music and More

In addition to music, Stirling has other interests that allow her to use her talents and hobbies. She has served as a Mormon missionary, is a philanthropist, writes musical arrangements for kids, and has published a best-selling book.

The Salt Lake Temple in Salt Lake City, Utah, is the largest Mormon temple in the world.

MISSIONARY DAYS

Before Stirling became successful, she served as a missionary for the Church of Jesus Christ of Latter-Day Saints. For a year and a half, Stirling worked to teach the Gospel of Christ to people in New York City. "This was a big sacrifice, but it was so worth it," she told Jake Healey of *LDS Living*. "I had to reach down inside myself and realize that there is more to me than my desires, my style, and my hobbies. God helped me discover a new side of myself."

Stirling failed to teach anyone for the first six months of her missionary work. She felt like a failure because she had worked hard but did not see any results. Later on, Stirling did help a man to find faith. He called Stirling an angel he met on the subway. She also taught a teenage boy how to pray who did not know how.

Stirling did find time to work on her music but did not achieve any success. Yet, Stirling says that her experience in New York City was the start of her career. She learned patience and polished her social skills. The negative comments and rejection she faced during her mission helped her develop a thick skin. It also made Stirling determined to forge ahead and succeed in the music business.

A BEST-SELLING AUTHOR

Stirling can add best-selling author to her list of accomplishments. Her autobiography, *The Only Pirate at the Party*, was released on January 12, 2016. She coauthored it with her younger sister, Brooke S. Passey. Stirling writes openly about her experiences in life and in her career and how they have shaped her as a person. Stirling also gives credit to her family members and friends, who have made a difference in her life and her success. On January 31, 2016, the book made the *New York Times* best-seller list.

WRITING MUSIC

Stirling's success has encouraged young people to learn to play the violin. She advises them to practice the scales even though

THE ONLY PIRATE AT THE PARTY

Stirling's first book is a memoir of her childhood and career. Often, she would write it after an exhausting show late at night and wherever she happened to be on tour. Stirling tells funny stories about growing up and about her early days in the music business. On her first day of kindergarten, Stirling dressed herself in a kimono and a curly brown wig. When she walked the red carpet for the first time at an event, she was unprepared and wore leg warmers and an old pair of sneakers. Included are childhood snapshots and a section of photos from Stirling's concerts. Stirling makes a dedication to Jason Gaviati, her band and tour member who passed away before the book was published.

Young fans meet Lindsey Stirling during a book signing event for *The Only Pirate at the Party* in Austin, Texas, on January 16, 2016.

it might be boring and then they can play what they want. Stirling has published books of musical arrangements specifically geared for kids to follow. They include cover songs and a medley of music from stage shows like *Phantom of the Opera*. They also come with music for the piano and CDs of backtracks to accompany the violin playing. Young musicians can get sheet music of Stirling's original songs to play. Stirling has been writing original music since she was in the band Stomp on Melvin in high school. Stirling says that she writes different styles of music, but with emotions and themes. She composes in an unstructured way and just as it comes to her.

Lindsey Stirling rehearses for the Cirque du Soleil fundraising event at the Mandalay Bay Resort and Casino in Las Vegas, Nevada, on March 20, 2014.

PHILANTHROPY

Stirling helps others by taking part in humanitarian causes that are important to her. In October 2013, Stirling joined a fund-raiser for the Atlanta Music Project in Atlanta, Georgia. The organization gives children of limited opportunities the chance to experience music and perform in choirs and orchestras. Stirling remembers how important music was to her as a child and how much she wanted to learn violin. "It breaks my heart that not everybody gets that chance to have music lessons or musical instruments to play and more and more schools are cutting programs, and that's why I teamed up with the Atlantic Music Project," Stirling explained to Abby Stevens of the *Deseret News*. For the fund-raiser, Stirling provided limited-edition T-shirts with her signature and the logo the Power of Music. The money raised helped the Atlanta Music Project reach the goal of giving musical training for fifty children.

In March 2014, Stirling performed with Cirque du Soleil at a fund-raiser in Las Vegas. The Canadian entertainment company puts on an annual stage show called *One Night for One Drop*. The money raised from ticket sales helps people to have access to clean and safe water worldwide. Artists from across the entertainment industry perform in the shows, which have raised more than $25 million.

Stirling has also performed at a charity event for breast cancer and raised money to help her bandmate Jason Gaviati during his cancer treatments. She has played her violin for patients at children's hospitals. During a tour in Africa, Stirling visited Kenya. She made a video of her visit to a rural community, where she played violin at a school, played with the children, visited their homes, learned their tribal dances, and dressed in native costume. Stirling even showed a tribal member how to hold and play her violin.

CHAPTER SIX

The Personal Side

M usic is important to Stirling, but she credits her personal life and experiences for making her who she is. Even more important than fame or success is her family and friends and her faith in God and her church.

ROLE OF FAITH IN STIRLING'S LIFE

Stirling is a Mormon, a member of the Church of Jesus Christ of Latter-Day Saints. Her religious faith and beliefs are a large part of her life. She credits God with surrounding her with amazing people who have helped her during personal challenges and throughout her musical career.

Stirling says that her career path has been directed by God. Even the results of her humiliating performance on *America's Got Talent* was part of God's plan. She told Morgan Jones of *Deseret News*, "I knew what I wanted; I was working so hard for it. I felt like I deserved it, but then I fell on my face. And that was God directing my path to a career, to a path that was so much better for me. I can look back on my own life and see how he has directed me, and it gives me hope and clarity for my future."

ROLE OF FAITH IN STIRLING'S MUSIC

Sometimes it's a challenge for Stirling to stay true to her faith in the world of pop culture. She works with designers to keep her show costumes modest, especially the necklines and sleeves. Stirling doesn't drink alcohol and avoids parties where there is a lot of drinking. Even when she's on a concert tour, Stirling tries to go to church.

Lindsey Stirling kicks her concert into high gear at the Citibank Hall in Sao Paulo, Brazil, on August 25, 2017.

Stirling has turned down offers to work with some well-known artists because their music or videos were crude and went against her moral standards. That was especially hard to do in the early days of Stirling's career when she would have liked the professional exposure.

CHALLENGES IN LIFE

Stirling's personal life has been affected by what she says was a "dark" time. In November 2015, her best friend and the keyboard player in her band, Jason "Gavi" Gaviati, died of cancer. He had played with Stirling since her very first concert tour. Soon after Gavi's death, Stirling's father, Stephen J. Stirling, was diagnosed with cancer. Her father passed away in January 2017. "Sometimes when you least expect it, life changes and life hits you," Stirling said to Morgan Jones of *Deseret News*. "I just had some things that I went through that really reminded me that none of this matters—no money, no amount of fame. What's important is the people around me." To get through these difficult times, Stirling relied on her religious faith. She read passages in scripture about the afterlife that teach about one day seeing again those loved ones who have passed on.

Losing two important people in her life had a strong impact on Stirling's music. The songs she wrote at the time were dark and depressing. They did not have any real depth, and Stirling realized that to write about her emotions she had to deal with them first. She shared these emotions in her 2016 album *Brave Enough*.

A HEALTH BATTLE

In her early twenties, Stirling struggled with the eating disorder anorexia nervosa. She also suffered from depression. Stirling's choices about how to eat or not to eat took over her life. Eventually, she realized that it also made her very unhappy. Publicly admitting that she had anorexia and using it in her music helped Stirling to work through her health battle.

ANOREXIA NERVOSA

Anorexia nervosa is a type of eating disorder. It is quite common and more than two hundred thousand cases are diagnosed in the United States each year. More girls and women struggle with it than men. Well-known people who have had eating disorders include Hilary Duff, Kesha, and Demi Lovato.

Symptoms of anorexia include body weight that is abnormally low. Anorexics are obsessive about how much they weigh and what and how much they eat. They might exercise too much to stay too thin. Treatment includes counseling and therapy. Hospitalization is sometimes required for anorexics to regain their normal body weight. If not treated, serious complications of anorexia include malnutrition and organ failure.

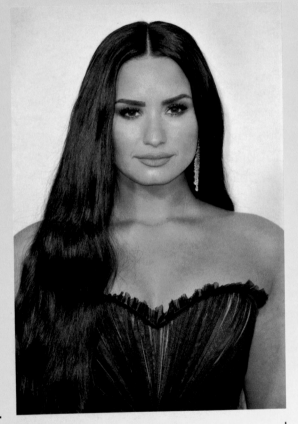

Singer Demi Lovato, who struggles with an eating disorder, is photographed at the American Music Awards in Los Angeles, California, on November 19, 2017.

Stirling's song "Shatter Me," from her album of the same name, is about her struggles with anorexia. She also tells her story in the video for the song. "It's symbolic of feeling trapped in an emotional box. Which is what I once had—I once had anorexia, and 'Shatter Me' is all about this ballerina and this music box, which represents me being stuck inside this mental disease and wanting to break free and crying out for help and finally having the courage to break free," she told John J. Moser of the *Morning Call*.

LOOKING TO THE FUTURE

Stirling has become successful in the music world by forging her own path. She continues to think outside the box and is not afraid to try new things. As actress Lucille Ball, one of Stirling's idols, said, "I'd rather regret the things I've done than regret the things I haven't done." In the coming years, Stirling would like to tour less and have a family someday. She dreams of having a show on Broadway and in Las Vegas. It would give her a permanent base to raise a family so she could continue to write music and perform it her way.

TIMELINE

1986 Stirling is born on September 21.

2002 Stirling joins the rock band Stomp on Melvin.

2007 On May 20, Stirling launches her YouTube channel, lindseystomp.

2010 On April 27, Stirling is a quarterfinalist on *America's Got Talent*.

2011 Stirling releases her first music video for her song "Spontaneous Me" on May 18.

2012 Stirling releases the music video for her song "Crystallize." It becomes the eighth-most-viewed video on YouTube with more than one hundred million views. Stirling's debut album, *Lindsey Stirling*, is released on September 18. On September 22, Stirling begins her first world concert tour.

2013 On January 25, Stirling admits to battling anorexia nervosa. On October 1, Stirling joins with the Atlanta Music Project to bring music appreciation to children. Stirling performs on the talk show *Conan* on October 24. Stirling and the group Pentatonix win a YouTube award for their version of the song "Radioactive" on November 3.

2014 Stirling releases her second album, *Shatter Me*. It posts at number two on the Billboard pop album chart. Stirling performs with Cirque du Soleil to celebrate World Water Day on March 22. Stirling kicks off her second world tour on May 13. Stirling is nominated for a Teen Choice Award.

2015 Lindseystomp reaches six million subscribers on January 19. Stirling wins Artist of the Year in the YouTube Awards on March 23. *Shatter Me* wins Top Dance/Electronic Album at the Billboard Music Awards on May 17. In August, Stirling graduates from Brigham Young University.

2016 Stirling's autobiography, *The Only Pirate at the Party*, is released on January 12. On January 31, the hardcover makes the best-seller list for nonfiction. Stirling releases her third album, *Brave Enough*, on August 19. Stirling begins her third concert tour.

2017 *Brave Enough* wins Top Dance/Electronic Album at the Billboard Music Awards on May 21. The YouTube documentary about Stirling, *Brave Enough*, debuts on September 5. On October 20, Stirling releases her fourth album, *Warmer in the Winter*. Stirling finishes second on *Dancing with the Stars* on November 21.

2018 Stirling appears at the Alaska State Fair on September 3. Stirling begins The Wanderland Tour on November 23 to mark the rerelease of her 2017 holiday album *Warmer in the Winter*.

GLOSSARY

anorexia nervosa An eating disorder marked by obsessive thoughts about weight and diet.

autobiography A person's life story written by that person.

backtracks Recorded music that is played along with a live musical performance.

choreography The arrangement of steps or moves for a performance.

cover song A recording or performance of a song by someone other than the original artist.

cross-dominance A learning disability marked by how the brain processes information.

debut The first appearance of a product.

dubstep A type of electronic dance music that emerged in the late 1990s.

dyslexia A learning disorder that makes it hard to read or understand written words.

gospel A religious teaching or belief.

kimono A robe-like garment originally worn in Japan.

memoir The story of someone's emotions and memories.

missionary A person who goes on a mission to promote a religion through education and service.

Mormon A person belonging to the Church of Jesus Christ of Latter-Day Saints.

open-mic An event where nonprofessional entertainers can perform.

philanthropy The donation or raising of money for a worthy cause.

platform A space to bring attention to one's work through social media and other ways.

scales (musical) A set order of musical notes according to pitch.

Scripture The books of the Bible.

stereotype A belief or an idea about a person, thing, or place.

FOR MORE INFORMATION

IMDB (Lindsey Stirling's page)
Website: https://www.imdb
.com/name/nm4826530
Stirling's page on the movie,
television, and video online
database IMDB has trivia,
quotes, photos, and information on her appearances.

Lindsey Stirling
Website: https://www.youtube
.com/user/lindseystomp
Stirling's YouTube channel has
music videos, collaborations
with other artists, videos
from concert tours, and the
documentary *Brave Enough*.

Lindsey Stirling Official Website
Website: http://www
.lindseystirling.com
Facebook: @lindseystirlingmusic
Twitter and Instagram:
@lindseystirling
YouTube: Lindsey Stirling
Stirling's website lists her
upcoming tour dates and
where to buy her music. It
also includes links to photos,

videos, and other information.

LindseyTime
Website: https://www.youtube
.com//user/LindseyTime
This YouTube channel has more
personal uploads,
like Stirling's skin care secret
and behind-the-scenes videos.

**Smithsonian National Museum
of American History**
Constitution Avenue NW
Between 12th and 14th Streets
Washington, DC 20560
(202) 633-1000
Website: http://americanhistory
.si.edu
Facebook: @americanhistory
Twitter: @amhistorymuseum
YouTube: National Museum of
American History
The shirt worn by Lindsey Stir-
ling in her breakout video
"Crystallize" is in the collec-
tion of this museum.

YouTube

901 Cherry Avenue
San Bruno, CA
(650) 253-0000
Website: https://www.youtube
.com
Facebook, Twitter, and
Instagram: @YouTube
YouTube is a video-sharing
website founded in 2005. It
is now part of Google.

Violin Lab

Email: violinlab@gmail.com
Website: http://violinlab.com
Teach yourself the violin
through online videos
offered here.

FOR FURTHER READING

DK. *Video Ideas: Full of Awesome Ideas to Try Out Your Video-Making Skills*. London, UK: DK Children, 2018.

Furgang, Adam. *20 Great Career-Building Activities Using You-Tube*. New York, NY: Rosen Publishing, 2017.

Hall, Kevin. *Creating and Building Your Own YouTube Channel*. New York, NY: Rosen Publishing, 2017.

Juilly, Brett. *Make Your Own Amazing YouTube Videos: Learn to Film, Edit, and Upload Quality Videos to YouTube*. New York, NY: Racehorse for Young Readers, 2017.

McAneney, Caitie. *Online Safety: Let's Talk About It*. New York, NY: Rosen Publishing, 2015.

Stirling, Lindsey. *Lindsey Stirling Favorites: Violin Play-Along*. Milwaukee, WI: Hal Leonard, 2016.

Stirling, Lindsey, and Brooke S. Passey. *The Only Pirate at the Party*. New York, NY: Gallery Books, 2016.

Tashjian, Janet, and Jake Tashjian. *My Life as a YouTuber*. New York, NY: Henry Holt and Co., 2018.

Willoughby, Nick. *Digital Filmmaking for Kids*. Hoboken, NJ: John Wiley & Sons, 2015.

Willoughby, Nick. *Making YouTube Videos: Star in Your Own Video*. Hoboken, NJ: John Wiley & Sons, 2016.

BIBLIOGRAPHY

Admin. "Lindsey Stirling Talks Competing on DanceOn's 'Dance Showdown' Season 3, New Album." NewMediaRockstars .com, October 30, 2013. http://newmediarockstars .com/2013/10/lindsey-stirling-talks-competing-on -danceons-dance-showdown-season-3-new-album -interview.

Collins, Simon. "Classical Crossover Queen Silences Critics." *Western Australian*, April 4, 2017. https://www.google .com/amp/s/thewest.com.au/entertainment/classical -crossover-queen-silences-critics-ng-b88423583z.amp.

Cutforth, Dan, and Jane Lipsitz. *Brave Enough*. Magical Elves Productions and YouTube Red, 2017.

DeMers, Jayson. "7 Reasons to Start a YouTube Channel Now (and the First Steps to Take)." *Forbes*, May 30, 2018. https:// www.forbes.com/sites/jaysondemers/2018/05/30/7-reasons -to-start-a-youtube-channel-now-and-first-steps-to take.

Fairley, James Dean. "The Pros and Cons of YouTube Business Marketing." LinkedIn, March 31, 2015. https://www.linkedin .com/pulse/pros-cons-youtube-business-marketing-james -dean-fairley.

Healey, Jake. "5 Famous Mormons Who Served Missions (& Where)." *LDS Living*, July 16, 2015. https://ldsmissionaries .com/5-famous-mormons-who-served-missions-where.

Jones, Morgan. "Dancing Violinist Lindsey Stirling Discusses Her New Book, LDS Faith and Taking a Different Route to Stardom." *Deseret News*, January 15, 2016. https://www .deseretnews.com/article/865645484/Dancing-violinist -Lindsey-Stirling-discusses her-new-book-LDS-faith-and -taking-an-untraditional.html.

Kain, Erik. "The Dancing Violinist: How Lindsey Stirling Is Con-
quering YouTube One Video At a Time." *Forbes*, August 29,
2012. https://www.forbes.com/sites/erikkain/2012/08/29
/the-dancing-violinist-how-lindsey-stirling-is-conquering
-youtube-one-video-at-a-time/#6993ad633baa.

Keller, Michael H. "The Flourishing Business of Fake YouTube
Views." *New York Times*, August 11, 2018. https://www
.nytimes.com/interactive/2018/08/11/technology/youtube
-fake-view-sellers.html.

Krewen, Nick. "Violinist Lindsey Stirling Credits YouTube with
Meteoric Rise." *Toronto Star*, June 13, 2014. https://www
.thestar.com/entertainment/music/2014/06/13/violinist
_lindsey_stirling_credits_youtube_with_meteoric_rise.html.

LDS Living staff. "Lindsey Stirling Passed Up Collaboration with
Big Stars Because of Her Standards." *LDS Living*, April 2013.
http://www.ldsliving.com/Lindsey-Stirling-Passed
-Up-Collaboration-with-Big-Stars-Because-of-Her
-Standards/s/81863.

Moser, John J. "Fiddling with Convention: Dancing violin virtuoso
Lindsey Stirling, coming to Sands, is high octane, joyous and
hip." *Morning Call*, July 27, 2018. http://www.mcall.com
/entertainment/lehigh-valley-music/mc-ent-lindsey-stirling
-interview-sands-bethlehem-20180720-story.html.

Niles, Laurie. "Violinist.com Interview with Lindsey Stirling: The
Scene in the Song." Violinist.com, October 1, 2014. https://
www.violinist.com/blog/laurie/201410/16239.

Philipkoski, Kristen. "Why Not Winning America's Got Talent
and Avoiding a Major Record Label Was Awesome for
Lindsey Stirling." *Forbes*, August 31, 2015. https://www
.forbes.com/sites/kristenphilipkoski/2015/08/31/hy-not
-winning-americas-got-talent-and-avoiding-a-major
-record-label-was-awesome-for-lindsey-stirling
/#5ec7da0c73a5.

Sharf, Samantha. "The 11 Best Pieces Of Advice For All Millennials From The Under 30 Summit." *Forbes*, October 7, 2015. https://www.forbes.com/sites/samanthasharf/2015/10/07/the-11-best-pieces-of-advices-for-all-millennials-at-the-under-30-summit/#2e9862636c38.

Stevens, Abby. "Violinist Lindsey Stirling Backs Power of Music Fundraiser." *Deseret News*, October 3, 2013. https://www.deseretnews.com/article/865587591/Violinist-Lindsey-Stirling-backs-Power-of-Music-fundraiser.html.

Stirling, Lindsey, and Brooke S. Passey. *The Only Pirate at the Party*. New York: Gallery Books, 2016.

Templeton, David. "Lindsey Stirling on her 'Brave' New Album and the Power of Practice." *Strings*, August 25, 2016. http://stringsmagazine.com/lindsey-stirling-on-her-brave-New-album-and-the-power-of-practice.

Varga, George. "Lindsey Stirling Bows Way to the Top." *San Diego Union-Tribune*, May 13, 2014. https://www.sandiegouniontribune.com/entertainment/music/sdut-lindsey-stirling-interview-2014may13-htmlstory.html.

INDEX

ABOUT THE AUTHOR

Henrietta Toth has written several nonfiction books for children. She is an editor with twenty years of experience in academic publishing. She has learned a lot by working on books about many different topics. Now she has learned a lot about YouTube, but she is still just learning to play her violin.

PHOTO CREDITS

THE WORRY-FREE BAKERY

Treats without Oil and Butter

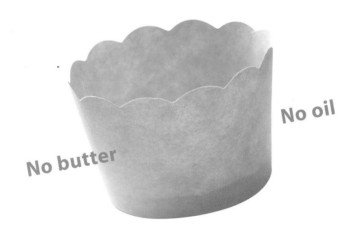

No butter

No oil

Kumiko Ibaraki

VERTICAL.

No butter, no oil—
nothing to worry about!

1 It's the same cake, but with less fat and fewer calories

When you first made cookies or a cake, weren't you surprised by the amount of butter the recipe called for? And if you eat something from a bakery it's hard to guess how much fat is actually in it. For example, did you know that a pound cake uses a pound each of flour, butter, sugar and eggs? A pound of butter is quite a lot. And that's what makes pound cake so rich.

Fats like butter are very high in calories and gram for gram have twice the energy compared to the same amount of a carboyhdrate. Also, our bodies burn calories from grains and carbohydrates first, so fats end up stored in the body. As a result, the more fat you consume the easier it is to gain weight. By eliminating the butter and oil, the recipes in this book are lower in total calories and have less fat.

2 Health Management and Disease Prevention

Gaining a few pounds is one thing, but gaining too much fat can lead to high levels of neutral fat and higher cholesterol as well. This can lead to hyperlipidemia and arteriosclerosis, as well as a higher risk of breast and colon cancer. There are also concerns about the medicine and feed given to cows that produce the milk for butter. The hormones and antibiotics given to livestock collects in the milk and body fat, as well as the heart. The same goes for fresh cream, cheese and high fat content dairy products.

Oil, too, is used in a variety of fried sweets, but the problem here is the way oil is produced, on top of the high fat content and calories. In the old days, oil was pressed from seeds, olives, etc. Now, however, chemicals are used to extract the oils and harmful residues remain in the finished product. For this reason, oil isn't be used.

Fats are found naturally in eggs, milk, sesame seeds and other items that will be used in this book. There's even a little natural oil in flour! The amount of fats in these ingredients is the right amount for your body. You'll get just the amount you need while still feeling satisfied.

3 Speed up your metabolism and get a naturally thin body

I always eat several servings of sweets every day. Sweets, cakes and snacks all tend to be associated with weight-gain. But if you don't use oil or butter and carefully choose your ingredients, the sweets are low in calories so they burn off quickly. You can enjoy feeding your hunger without the worry of gaining weight.

Eat when you get hungry— that's the key to revving up your metabolism and slimming down your body. Instead of three meals a day, eat five or six smaller meals to help speed up your metabolism. You'll digest more quickly and burn off calories instead of storing it away as fat. Conversely, if you were to go on a restricted diet with low calories or less food, your basal metabolism would slow down and, ironically, you'd end up storing fat more easily. If you eat more of the right kinds of foods your body will burn it up for energy instead of storing it. Creating a high-metabolism body is the best kind of diet there is.

4 Keeping the Sweet in Sweets

In my treats, I don't use oil or butter, but I do use sugar. Most people think of sugar as fattening, but it's okay. Your body burns it off fast so it's a safe ingredient to use. Your body can easily break down the sugar and convert it into energy. In fact, compared to other nutrients, sugar turns into energy the fastest.

Sugar is an important nutrient as an energy source for your brain and body. It helps raise serotonin levels in your brain, which helps stabilize your mood. So, with that knowledge, be at ease and make as many treats as you want for you and your family.

5 The cooking is easy and simple

Without oil and butter, the recipes become even easier to make. For example, normally with cake you need to wait for the butter to be at room temperature before mixing it with the sugar. Since I don't use butter in my recipe, you can skip right over to mixing the sugar with the eggs.

I don't use butter in pie or tart crusts, either. So whatever the recipe, it's even easier and less stressful to make.

6 Economical ingredients

Flour, sugar and eggs are less expensive than butter, cream, and cheese. If we eliminate those, the recipes are even less expensive to make. Instead, you can use the difference to buy good quality, organic products. Please take a look at page 76 for buying guides.

7 Clean up is so easy, the dishes almost wash themselves

Since there's no grease from oil or butter, washing bowls and utensils afterwards is a piece of cake. Items like hand mixers and whisks can be tough to clean, but soaking them in hot water will make clean-up easier. Using less dish soap means less of a burden on the environment—and that's always a good thing.

Contents

Dreamy Sweets

Cool Confections

Guides

■ Cooking times listed are for gas ovens.

■ Electric ovens require slightly longer cooking times.

■ The microwave times are for 500-watt microwaves.

■ Use medium-size eggs.

Because grams are a mass-based measurement, and each ingredient has a different mass, the conversion to US cups or tablespoons is different for each ingredient. The listed conversions hew as close to standard measurements as possible while preserving the original amount.

Everyday Treats

It's easy to make snacks for your kids or to go with a relaxing cup of tea. The best part is you'll rest easy knowing they're not fattening.

Apple Muffins
A light fluffiness without any butter

You can make delicious muffins without using any butter. The secret to a perfect fluffy muffin is milk and well-whisked eggs.

You can make a variety of muffins by substituting the apples for other fruits like sweetened chestnuts, or dried fruits like raisins and apricots. Even canned fruits are great for muffins.

Ingredients
(yields 10 2″ muffins)

- 1 apple (Jonathan or Jonagold)
- 1 Tbsp sugar
- Dash salt
- 1 C (130 g) cake flour (low gluten)
- 1/2 tsp baking powder
- 2 eggs
- 1/3 C (70 g) sugar
- 1/5 C (50 ml) milk
- Dash vanilla extract

Instructions

1. Peel skin off apple and cut lengthwise into 8ths. Cut 8ths into small pieces and sprinkle with salt. Place apples in microwave-safe bowl and cover with 1 Tbsp sugar. Microwave uncovered for 5 minutes. Remove from microwave and drain any liquid.

2. Sift together flour and baking powder.

3. In a bowl, combine egg and 1/3 C sugar, and whisk with a hand mixer.

4. Add milk and apples and gently mix with rubber spatula.

5. Add flour mixture and vanilla extract, then mix briefly.

6. Line trays with paper muffin cups and fill with mixture. Cook at 350°F (180°C) for 15 minutes. Poke a muffin with a toothpick to ensure it's fully cooked, then remove from oven. Let stand on a wire rack to cool.

Regular apple muffin 158 calories ➡ **Low-cal recipe** 111 calories

Chocolate Banana Muffins
Low in fat yet very delicious

Instead of baking chocolate and all those calories, I use cocoa to get that chocolate goodness. You'll know it's done when you get a whiff of the warm, baked bananas. If you have bananas left over you can always save them in the freezer.

Ingredients
(yields eight 2″ muffins)

2 bananas (about 5 1/4 oz)
⎡ 3/4 C (100 g) cake flour
⎢ 1/3 C (30 g) cocoa
⎣ 1/2 tsp baking soda
2 eggs
1/3 C (70 g) sugar
1/5 C (50 ml) milk
Dash vanilla extract
1 Tbsp rum

Instructions

1 Mash bananas with a whisk, then purée in a blender. Sift together flour, baking soda and cocoa.

2 In a bowl, combine eggs and sugar and whisk with a hand mixer until thickened.

3 Add bananas and milk. Stir with a rubber spatula.

4 Stir in flour mixture, vanilla extract and rum.

5 Line muffin tray with paper cups and pour batter into cups. Bake at 350°F (180°C) for 15 minutes. Remove and let cool. Garnish with powdered sugar if desired.

Regular chocolate muffin 197 calories ➡ Low-cal recipe 132 calories

Pumpkin Cakes
Load up the veggies and pile on the nutrition

Another muffin variation with a healthy twist.
I've added *kabocha* pumpkin to pump up the texture and
add some nutritionally balanced goodness.

Ingredients
(yields six 1 x 3 x 2" cakes)

5 oz (140 g) *kabocha* (or regular) pumpkin
1/5 C (50 ml) milk
⎡ 1 C (130 g) cake flour
⎢ 1/3 tsp cinnamon
⎣ 1/2 tsp baking powder
2 eggs
1/2 C (90 g) sugar
Dash vanilla extract
1 Tbsp rum
12 pumpkin seeds

Instructions

1 Dice pumpkin into 1" cubes and boil in water until soft. Drain, then mash with a whisk. Add milk and blend well.

2 Sift together flour, cinnamon and baking powder.

3 In a bowl, combine egg and sugar and whisk with a hand mixer until thickened.

4 Stir in pumpkin.

5 Add flour, vanilla extract and rum liquor and mix with rubber spatula.

6 Line six bread pans with parchment paper, pour mixture evenly into cups and place two pumpkin seeds on each loaf. Cook at 350°F (180°C) for 15 minutes.

Regular pumpkin cake 260 calories **Low-cal recipe** 180 calories

Crispy Scones
The hidden power of sesame

The secret to these scones' crunchy goodness is the starch and ground sesame. This is a tea time favorite at my house, and it's great for breakfast too. A scone that stands out even without butter and oil—try it with a pat of Non-Butter Spread.

Ingredients
(yields five 2" scones)

- 1 C + 1 tsp (140 g) cake flour (low gluten)
- 2 Tbsp (20 g) potato (or corn) starch
- 1 heaping Tbsp baking powder
- 2/5 tsp salt
- 1 egg yolk
- 1/5 C (40 g) sugar
- 1 Tbsp condensed milk
- 2 2/3 Tbsp milk
- 1/3 oz (10 g) ground sesame seeds
- Milk, for basting

Instructions

1 Sift together flour, potato starch, baking powder and salt.

2 In a bowl, combine egg yolk, sugar, and condensed milk, then whisk.

3 Add milk slowly as you whisk. Add flour and sesame and stir with chopping motions with a plastic card or spatula.

4 Remove mixture from bowl and press out to form a mound 2/3" thick. It's okay if it's clumpy.

5 Use a circular mold or cup 2" in diameter to cut out 5 rounds. Place scones on a parchment-lined baking sheet. Cook at 350°F (180°C) for 15 minutes.

Regular scone 271 calories ➡ **Low-cal recipe** 189 calories

Non-Butter Spread

For the times you crave butter, try this low-cal alternative on your toast or pancakes. It has 1/7 the calories of regular butter and can be refrigerated for 3 to 4 days. You can freeze it, too.

Ingredients
(yields 2/3 C (140 g))

1 egg yolk
2 tsp (5 g) cake flour (low gluten)
1/3 C (90 ml) milk
Pinch salt
⌐ 1/2 tsp (1 g) powdered gelatin
└ 1 tsp water
1 Tbsp plain yogurt

Instructions

1 Combine gelatin and water.

2 In a bowl, combine egg yolk and flour, and whisk. Slowly add milk while whisking, then pour into a small pot.

3 Add salt and bring to a boil over medium heat. Remove from heat. Add gelatin and mix. Stir in yogurt. Pour into a container, cover with plastic wrap and place in refrigerator.

Picture Pancakes
Made from scratch!

These pancakes are a standard at my house on holidays. Everyone likes to draw their own picture. These are filling and fluffy pancakes made with eggs and milk.

Ingredients
(yields six 6" pancakes)

- 1 C + 1 Tbsp (150 g) cake flour (low gluten)
- 2 tsp baking powder
- 1 egg
- 2 Tbsp (25 g) sugar
- 1/2 C milk
- 1/4 C water
- Dash vanilla extract
- 1 tsp cocoa

Instructions

1. Sift together baking powder and flour.

2. In a bowl, combine egg and sugar, and whisk until mixture turns light in color. Stir in milk and water.

3. Add flour and mix briefly. Stir in vanilla extract.

4. In a separate bowl, add 3 Tbsp of pancake mixture and cocoa, then blend. Follow instructions on page 75 to make a cornet. Fill cornet with cocoa batter.

5. In a warm pan, draw a picture using the cornet. Place a ladleful of batter on top. Cook over medium heat until small bubbles form on top of the pancake. Flip and cook until golden. Cook remaining pancakes in the same manner. Add maple syrup or try Non-Butter Spread from page 13.

Regular pancake 212 calories **Low-cal recipe** 134 calories

Strawberry Custard Crepe
Low cholesterol and low calorie custard

The secret to the creamy low calorie custard is using less egg yolk.
The warm crepe envelopes the sweet strawberry and creamy custard goodness.

Ingredients (yields 8)

16 small strawberries

Crepe Batter
1 light C (120 g) cake flour
  (low gluten)
1 egg
1 2/3 Tbsp (20 g) sugar
4/5 C milk
Dash vanilla extract

Custard
1 egg yolk
4 Tbsp (50 g) sugar
2 Tbsp cake flour
4/5 C milk
Dash each rum, vanilla extract

Instructions

1 Thinly slice the strawberries. Sift flour.

2 Make the crepe batter. In a bowl, combine egg
  and sugar, and whisk thoroughly. Add flour
  slowly and stir in milk. Add the vanilla extract
  and chill in refrigerator for 30 minutes.

3 While batter is chilling, make the custard. In
  a bowl, combine egg yolk, sugar, flour, a small
  amount of milk, and stir. Add remaining milk
  and pour custard into a pot. Bring to a boil over
  medium heat, stir occasionally, then turn off
  heat. Add vanilla extract and rum, pour into a
  container, cover with plastic wrap and let cool.

4 In a non-stick pan, pour chilled batter into a thin circle 8" in
  diameter. When one side is cooked, flip over and cook until golden.

5 Place crepe on a plate, add custard crème to center using a pastry
  bag, and lay strawberry slices on top. Fold together and serve.

Regular crepe 213 calories ➡ **Low-cal recipe** 153 calories

No-fry Donuts Not fried! Really!

Since my daughter loves donuts, I've been looking for ways to make them without having to deep-fry them. The magic behind these donuts is the rice flour sprinkled on when they go into the oven.

Ingredients (yields 9 donuts)

A
- 2/3 C (95 g) bread flour (high gluten)
- 2 1/2 Tbsp (20 g) cake flour (low gluten)
- 2 tsp dry yeast
- 2 1/2 Tbsp sugar
- 1/2 egg (25 g)
- 1/2 C (120 ml) milk (warmed to 100°F (40°C))

B
- 2/3 C (95 g) bread flour
- 1/3 tsp salt
- Dash lemon zest
- Dash vanilla extract

Rice flour, as needed
2 Tbsp granulated sugar
Cinnamon Sugar (3 Tbsp sugar + 1/5 tsp cinnamon)

Instructions

1 In a bowl, add mixture A and stir with a rubber spatula. Thoroughly mix in yeast.

2 Add mixture B and stir until no clumps remain.

3 When dough forms one large mass, remove from bowl and knead on a board or flat surface.

4 When dough is smooth, shape into a ball, place in a bowl cover with plastic wrap. Heat in oven at 100°F (40°C) for 25 minutes, or set aside in a warm area to allow dough to rise.

5 When the dough has doubled in size remove from oven. Press dough with fists to remove air and then reform into a ball. Cover with a slightly damp cloth and set aside for 10 minutes.

6 Dust work surface with rice flour. Use a rolling pin to roll dough into an 8" x 12" piece.

7 Cut donut shapes out of dough and line up on a parchment-lined tray along with donuts "holes." Take the remaining dough and reform into a bowl and place back in bowl and cover with a slightly damp cloth for 10 minutes. Roll out again and cut donuts from dough.

8 Sprinkle rice flour on donuts and again place in 100°F (40°C) oven for 20 minutes to rise.

9 Bake for 9 minutes at 350°F (180°C) and sprinkle with Cinnamon Sugar while warm. Garnish with granulated sugar if desired.

Regular donut 192 calories ➡ **Low-cal recipe** 134 calories

Chocolate Twists
**Handmade twists
without all the calories**

A rich chocolate spread over sweet pastry. Skipping the oil and using cocoa make this a great alternative to store-bought sweets. Be careful not to overdose on these goodies!

Ingredients
(yields 10 twists)

A
- 2/3 C (90 g) bread flour (high gluten)
- 2 Tbsp (15 g) cake flour (low gluten)
- 2 tsp dry yeast
- 2 1/2 Tbsp sugar
- 1/2 egg (25 g)
- 1/2 C milk (warmed to 100°F)

B
- 2/3 C (90 g) bread flour
- 3 3/4 Tbsp (20 g) cocoa
- 1/3 tsp salt
- Dash vanilla extract

Rice flour as needed

C
- 2 Tbsp sugar
- 1 Tbsp cocoa
- 1 tsp egg white

Instructions

1 In a bowl, add mixture A and stir with a rubber spatula. Thoroughly mix in yeast. Add mixture B and stir until no clumps remain. When dough forms one large mass, remove from bowl and knead on a board or flat surface.

2 When dough is smooth, shape into a ball, place in a bowl and cover with plastic wrap. Heat in oven at 100°F (40°C) for 25 minutes to let rise.

3 When dough has doubled in size, remove from oven and divide into ten equal-sized clumps. Roll into small balls and cover with a slightly damp cloth for 10 minutes.

4 Take each ball and roll out between palms into 8" long pieces. Fold in half and twist, then press ends together.

5 Place on parchment-lined tray and sprinkle rice flour on top. Place in 100°F (40°C) oven for 20 minutes to let rise.

6 Bake for 9 minutes at 350°F (180°C). Combine mixture C and spread onto twists.

Regular chocolate twist 200 calories ➡ **Low-cal recipe** 125 calories

Belgian Waffles
The final result of many trial recipes

Regular Belgian waffles are made with loads of butter.
After many trials, I've found the perfect low-fat version.
A good amount of milk makes for a filling meal.

Ingredients
(yields 5 waffles)

A
- 1/2 C (75 g) bread flour (high gluten)
- 1 tsp dry yeast
- 2 2/5 Tbsp (30 g) sugar
- 1 egg yolk
- 1/3 C milk (warmed to 100°F)

B
- 1/2 C (75 g) cake flour (low gluten)
- 1/5 tsp salt
- Dash vanilla extract

1 1/2 Tbsp granulated sugar

Instructions

1 In a bowl, combine mixture A. Thoroughly blend in yeast. Add mixture B and stir well. When dough forms one large mass, remove from bowl and knead on a board or flat surface.

2 When the dough is smooth, add granulated sugar and mix well. Place in a bowl and cover with plastic wrap. Place in oven at 100°F (40°C) and let dough rise.

3 When the dough has doubled in size, remove from oven and divide into 5 balls. Let sit for 5 minutes with a slightly damp cloth on top. Place dough back on tray and heat in 100°F (40°C) oven for another 20 minutes.

4 Remove from oven and cook dough on waffle maker. Cook for 3 minutes on each side on low to medium heat.

Regular waffle 251 calories Low-cal recipe 169 calories

Cherry Blossom Muffins
Light and fluffy!

This is a favorite snack at my house during *hanami*, or cherry blossom parties. Their one-of-a-kind taste comes from the steamed cherry blossom flowers. Just be sure not to oversteam them. The whisked eggs provide the perfect amount of fluff for this floral treat.

Ingredients
(yields six 2″ muffins)

6 salted cherry flowers
6 salted cherry leaves
2/5 C (60 g) cake flour (low gluten)
1 tsp baking powder
2 egg whites
2 Tbsp (25 g) sugar
2 egg whites
2 Tbsp (25 g) sugar
1 Tbsp milk
Dash vanilla extract

Instructions

1 Sift together flour and baking powder. Soak the cherry flowers and leaves in water to remove salt, then pat dry. Place 1 leaf in the bottom of each paper muffin cup.

2 In a bowl, add egg whites and whisk with a hand mixer while gradually adding sugar. Whisk until stiff peaks form.

3 In a separate bowl, combine egg yolks and sugar. Mix in egg whites with a rubber spatula.

4 Add sifted flour and baking powder, milk and vanilla extract, then stir.

5 Pour batter into muffin cups and place a cherry flower on each. Place in a steamer and steam for 15 minutes over low heat. Check with a toothpick; if it comes out clean, remove from steam and let cool.

Regular muffin 138 calories ➡ **Low-cal recipe** 83 calories

Cookie Cutter Cookies
No need to wait for any butter to melt

While my daughter loves to make animals and draw cute pictures, I like to make cool designs that adults can enjoy at tea time. Since there's no butter, you can easily save extra dough for another day, since it won't oxidize as quickly.

Ingredients
(yields 14 cookies)

⌐ 3/4 C (100 g) cake flour (low gluten)
└ 1/3 tsp baking powder
1 egg yolk
3 1/5 Tbsp (40 g) sugar
2 Tbsp condensed milk
1 to 2 Tbsp milk
Dash vanilla extract
Cake flour, for dusting
Beaten egg, for basting
A ⌐ 2/3 Tbsp sugar
  └ 1/2 tsp egg white

Instructions

1 Sift together flour and baking powder.

2 In a bowl, combine egg yolk and sugar and whisk until pale yellow.

3 Add condensed milk and flour and mix with a plastic card or spatula. Add milk gradually until dough forms a solid mass.

4 Transfer dough to a board or flat surface and add vanilla extract. Knead lightly and shape into a ball. Place in plastic bag and let sit for 5 minutes.

5 Sprinkle work surface with flour and roll out dough with a rolling pin until dough is 1/8" thick. Line tray with parchment paper. Cut out shapes from dough and place cookies on parchment-lined tray.

6 Baste cookies with beaten egg, then place in oven and bake for 6 minutes at 350°F (180°C).

7 Combine mixture A and make a cornet (see page 75) for piping. Remove cookies from oven and let stand on wire rack to cool. Decorate while still warm.

Regular cookie (2 per serving) 170 calories ➡ **Low-cal recipe** 122 calories

Cream Sandwich Cookies
Creamy goodness!

A raisin-dotted cream in a crunchy cookie shell—these are very stylish.
The dash of parmesan cheese adds a perfect twist to these cookies.

Ingredients
(yields 5 cookies)

- 1/2 C + 1 Tbsp (80 g)
  cake flour (low gluten)
- 1/5 tsp baking powder
- 1 egg yolk
- 2 Tbsp (25 g) sugar
- 1 Tbsp condensed milk
- 1 Tbsp milk
- Dash vanilla extract
- Cake flour, for dusting
- Beaten egg, for basting

A
- 1/3 C (90 g) plain yogurt
- 2 2/5 Tbsp (30 g) sugar
- 20 raisins (10 g)
- 2 tsp rum
- 1/2 tsp (1 g) grated
  Parmesan cheese

Instructions

1 Drain plain yogurt overnight, then wrap in fresh paper towels and press (see page 74). You should end up with about 2 Tbsp (30 g).

2 Sift together flour and baking powder. Soak raisins in rum.

3 In a bowl, combine egg yolk and sugar and whisk until light in color. Stir in condensed milk.

4 Add flour and mix lightly with a plastic card or spatula. Add milk and stir until dough forms one large mass.

5 Transfer dough to a board or flat surface and add vanilla extract. Knead lightly and shape into a ball. Place in plastic bag and let sit for 5 minutes.

6 Sprinkle work surface with flour and roll out dough using a rolling pin until it's 1/8" thick. Line tray with parchment paper. Cut out 10 rectangles 1 3/4" x 2 1/2" (4.5 x 6.5 cm) from dough and place cookies on lined tray. Poke holes with a fork and baste with beaten egg. Bake at 350°F (180°C) for 12 minutes.

7 Combine mixture A. When cookies have cooled, spread cream mixture on one cookie and press another cookie on top.

Regular cream cookie 242 calories ➡ **Low-cal recipe** 144 calories

Florentines
High calories treats turned healthy

A lot of butter and oil is used when making florentines,
but instead I use milk and syrup, and top them off with toasted almonds.

Ingredients
(makes one 8″ square piece)

- 1 light C (120 g) cake flour (low gluten)
- 1/3 tsp baking powder
- 1 small egg (40 g)
- 4 Tbsp (50 g) sugar
- Cake flour, for dusting
- A
  - 4 1/5 Tbsp (80 g) condensed milk
  - 1 1/2 Tbsp (30 g) each starch syrup, honey
  - 1 oz (30 g) sliced almonds

Instructions

1. Place almonds on baking tray and bake in oven at 340°F (170°C) for 5 minutes. Sift together flour and baking powder. Line an 8" baking sheet with parchment paper.

2. In a bowl, combine egg and sugar and whisk. Add flour and mix with chopping motions with a plastic card or spatula. Transfer to a flat surface and knead gently, then place dough in a plastic bag and set aside for 10 minutes.

3. Sprinkle flour over work surface and roll out dough into a 8" square. Place dough in baking pan and poke holes with a fork. Bake at 350°F (180°C) for 5 minutes.

4. In a small pot, add condensed milk, starch syrup and honey. Simmer over medium heat and stir until creamy. Add almonds and mix.

5. When dough is done baking, pour almond mixture on top and place back in oven to bake for 10 minutes. Remove from oven and let cool. Remove Florentine from pan and cut into 8 pieces.

Regular Florentine (1/8 piece) 271 calories ➡ **Low-cal recipe** 166 calories

Chocolate Flake Clusters
Cocoa at its best!

Everyone loves those chocolate flakes from the store,
so here's a homemade version that's lighter in calories.
If you don't tell your guests, they won't notice the difference.

Ingredients
(yields 15 clusters)

2 C (50 g) corn flakes

A
- 1 egg white
- 2 2/5 Tbsp (30 g) sugar
- 2 Tbsp cocoa, sifted
- 1 Tbsp condensed milk
- 1/2 Tbsp (10 g) starch syrup

Instructions

1 Add mixture A to a small pot and stir over medium heat until thickened. Remove from heat, add corn flakes and stir quickly.

2 Line pan with parchment paper. Using 2 spoons, make 15 small chocolate clusters.

3 Bake in oven at 350°F (180°C) for 12 to 13 minutes. Remove and let cool on a wire rack.

Regular clusters (3 per serving) 159 calories ➡ **Low-cal recipe** 90 calories

Shortbread Biscuits
Without the calories of shortening!

The taste of ordinary shortbread cookies comes from
the high-fat content shortening that's usually used.
Here, I've used rice flour for a perfect low-fat tea time snack.

Ingredients
(yields one 7″ pie)

A
- 2/3 C (90 g) cake
  flour (low gluten)
- 1/5 C (30 g) rice flour
- 1/2 tsp baking powder
- 1/5 tsp salt

1 egg yolk
4 2/5 Tbsp (55 g) sugar

B
- 1 Tbsp (20 g)
  condensed milk
- 1 Tbsp milk

Dash vanilla extract
Flour, for dusting
Milk, for basting
1/2 Tbsp granulated sugar

Instructions

1 Sift together mixture A.

2 In a bowl, combine egg yolk and sugar and whisk.
  Add mixture B and stir.

3 Add sifted flour and stir with chopping motions
  with a plastic card or spatula. Stir in vanilla extract.

4 Transfer to a flat surface and knead gently, then put
  in a plastic bag and set aside for 10 minutes.

5 Sprinkle flour over work surface and roll out dough
  into a 7" circle. Place on parchment-lined baking
  sheet. Baste with milk and sprinkle sugar on top.

6 Poke holes in dough with a fork to make perfora-
  tions for six slices. Bake at 350°F (180°C) for 20
  minutes. Remove from oven and let stand. Cut
  biscuits while warm.

Regular biscuit (1/6 piece) 220 calories **Low-cal recipe** 134 calories

Burdock and Carrot Cake
A nutritious bread-like cake that's even good for breakfast

Most people are pretty surprised to see burdock used in a cake, but vanilla, burdock and brandy blend together flawlessly. I soak the vegetables in water so they're tender enough for this sweet breakfast-ready cake.

Ingredients
(yields four 4″ x 2″ cakes)

1/2 C (60 g) chopped carrots
1/3 C (40 g) burdock root
A ⎧ 3 Tbsp sugar
⎪ 1 Tbsp brandy
⎩ Dash vanilla extract
B ⎧ 1 C (130 g) cake flour (low gluten)
⎪ 1/2 tsp baking powder
⎩ 1/2 tsp salt
2 eggs
1/2 C (70 g) unpacked brown sugar
2 2/3 Tbsp (50 g) condensed milk
Dash vanilla extract

Instructions

1 In a food processor, mince burdock and carrot. Soak in water to remove bitterness, then drain. Place in a microwave-safe bowl, cover with plastic wrap and heat for 5 minutes. Combine mixture A in a bowl. Drain water from vegetables and add to mixture A. Set aside for 1 hour to marinate.

2 Sift together mixture B. Line cake trays with baking cups.

3 In a bowl, combine eggs and brown sugar, then whisk using a hand mixer until thickened.

4 Add vegetable mixture from step 1 and stir with a rubber spatula. Add condensed milk and stir. Stir in sifted flour and vanilla extract.

5 Pour into lined trays. Bake at 350°F (180°C) for 20 minutes.

Regular carrot cake (1/2 loaf) 240 calories ➡ **Low-cal recipe** 162 calories

Lemon Chiffon Cake
Worry-free lemon-flavored goodness

Lemon Chiffon is my pride and joy dish, it bakes so well, you'll never miss the oil or butter. People often ask what I use to replace the fatty ingredients, but there's nothing. It's just perfectly balanced. To make it picture-perfect, I use a paper pan liner.

Ingredients
(yields one 7″ cake)

4 egg whites
2 4/5 Tbsp (35 g) sugar
4 egg yolks
2 4/5 Tbsp (35 g) sugar
A ⌐ 1 2/3 Tbsp (25 ml) lemon juice
⌐ 2 1/3 Tbsp (35 ml) water
Lemon zest (from 1/2 lemon)
1/2 C flour, sifted

Instructions

1 In a bowl, whisk egg whites with a hand mixer. Add sugar gradually. Continue to whisk until stiff peaks form.

2 In a separate bowl, add egg yolks and sugar, and whisk on low using a hand mixer until pale yellow. Add mixture A and lemon zest and mix thoroughly on low.

3 Add flour and mix on low speed. Add egg whites gradually and mix with a rubber spatula. Pour batter back into the first bowl and stir well.

4 Add batter to a paper-lined tube pan and cook at 320°F (160°C) for 30 minutes. After 6 or 7 minutes in the oven, remove and make 4 shallow incisions on cake. This will help the cake rise evenly while baking. Place back in oven for 23 minutes (total cooking time: 30 minutes).

5 Use a bottle as a balance and invert cake for half a day.

6 Carefully remove from pan (see page 75). Garnish with sugar or lemon slices if desired.

Regular lemon chiffon cake (1/8 cake) 184 calories ➡ **Low-cal recipe** 111 calories

Chocolate Chiffon Cake
Fragrant chocolate will entice you!

Like the lemon chiffon, this is another light and fluffy cake. I've replaced all the high-calorie baking chocolate with cocoa. You can make one big 7" cake instead of four small ones.

Ingredients
(yields four 4″ cakes)

- 4 egg whites
- 2 4/5 Tbsp (35 g) sugar
- 4 egg yolks
- 2 4/5 Tbsp (35 g) sugar
- 1/4 C milk
- 2/5 C (55 g) cake flour (low gluten)
- 3 3/4 Tbsp cocoa
- Dash vanilla extract

Instructions

1 In a bowl, whisk egg whites with a hand mixer. Add sugar gradually. Whisk until stiff peaks form.

2 In a separate bowl, add egg yolks and sugar, and whisk on low speed until pale yellow. Stir in milk.

3 Add flour and vanilla extract, then mix on low speed. Add whisked egg whites gradually while mixing with a rubber spatula. Pour batter back into the first bowl and stir.

4 Add batter to paper-lined cake pans and cook at 320°F (160°C) for 30 minutes. After 6 or 7 minutes in the oven, remove and make 4 shallow incisions on each cake. This will help the cake rise evenly while baking. Place back in oven for remaining 13 minutes (total baking time: 20 minutes).

5 Use a bottle as a balance and invert cake for half a day.

6 Carefully remove from tray (see page 75). Garnish with confectioner's sugar if desired.

Regular chocolate chiffon cake (1/2 cake) 180 calories **Low-cal recipe** 113 calories

Omelet Crepes
Crepes for people on a diet

This is a staple menu item at my shop. A light mix with creamy custard and fruits wrapped like a bouquet of flowers.

Ingredients
(yields 6 crepes)

Omelet Mix
- 2 egg whites
- 2 2/5 Tbsp (30 g) sugar
- 2 egg yolks
- 1 Tbsp (20 g) starch syrup
- 1 Tbsp + 1 tsp (20 ml) milk
- 1 Tbsp (20 g) condensed milk
- 3 Tbsp (25 g) cake flour (low gluten)
- 1 1/4 Tbsp (10 g) bread flour (high gluten)

Custard crème filling: see page 15
12 slices banana, cut on the bias
Sliced almonds and confectioner's sugar, as needed

Instructions

1 Sift both flours together.

2 In a microwave-safe dish, combine starch syrup and milk, and heat for 20 seconds. Stir in condensed milk.

3 Place sliced almonds on a baking dish and bake for 10 minutes at 340°F (170°C). Line tray with parchment paper and draw three 6" circles.

4 In a bowl, whisk egg whites with a hand mixer and add sugar gradually until stiff peaks form.

5 In a separate bowl, add egg yolks and syrup mixture, and whisk on low speed using a hand mixer. Whisk in flour.

6 Slowly add egg white meringue to batter from step 5 while stirring with rubber spatula. Spoon batter onto tray and make 6 even circles. Bake at 350°F (180°C) for 12 minutes. Remove from oven and place each crepe in a plastic bag to cool.

7 Make custard crème (see page 15).

8 Slice crepes in half. Fill middle of crepes with custard, bananas and almonds. Fold and garnish with confectioner's sugar.

Regular omelet crepe 250 calories ➡ **Low-cal recipe** 183 calories

Apple Pie A standard in low-fat treats!

A low-calorie treat five years in the making. We were so happy to have perfected this recipe that my staff and I were hugging one another. The key is the yogurt—it helps give the crust its crispy texture. Be sure to use Jonathan or Jonagold apples!

Ingredients (yields one 4 3/4" x 10" pie)

Pie Crust
- 3/4 C (100 g) cake flour (low gluten)
- 2 Tbsp potato (or corn) starch
- 1/2 tsp baking powder
- 2/5 tsp salt
- 4/5 C (200 g) plain yogurt
- 1 egg yolk
- 1 1/3 Tbsp (20 ml) milk
- Flour, for dusting

Filling
- 1 medium apple (appx. 5 oz (150 g))
- 2 Tbsp granulated sugar
- Cinnamon to taste

Beaten egg, for basting
1 Tbsp apricot jam

Instructions

1 Drain plain yogurt overnight, then wrap in fresh paper towels and press (refer to page 74). You should end up with appx. 1/3 C (70 g).

2 Peel apple, then slice into thin wedges. Place apple slices in a microwave-safe bowl. Add sugar and cinnamon, and stir. Heat for 5 minutes, then drain any liquid.

3 Sift together flour, potato starch, baking powder and salt. Add drained yogurt and mix with chopping motions with a plastic card or spatula. Stir in blended egg yolk and milk. Place dough in plastic bag and set aside for 10 minutes.

4 Sprinkle flour on a board or flat surface and roll out dough, fold into thirds and flip over to roll out again. Fold in thirds and return to plastic bag for 10 minutes.

5 Roll out dough into a rectangle 10 1/4" in length. Slice dough in half lengthwise, with one piece 2/5" (1 cm) wider than the other.

6 Arrange apple slices on the narrower piece dough. Take the wider piece of dough and fold in half lengthwise. Make small slices 2/5" apart while leaving a margin around the edges.

7 Baste apples and dough edges with egg. Place scored dough over apples with the fold along the middle, then unfold and align edges. Press edges of dough together with a fork. Make sure edges are sealed by basting again with egg.

8 Place on parchment-lined baking sheet and bake at 350°F (180°C) for 25 minutes. Remove from oven and coat with apricot jam while still warm.

Everyday Treats

Regular apple pie (1/6 pie) 344 calories ➡ **Low-cal recipe** 121 calories

Heart Palmier
A little low-calorie love

Since I don't use any butter for these treats, you don't have to refrigerate the dough as you make them, even during summer. These are the easiest little goodies to make, so spread the love!

Ingredients
(yields 15 cookies)

- 1/2 C + 1 Tbsp (80 g) cake flour (low gluten)
- 1 1/2 Tbsp potato (or corn) starch
- 1/3 tsp baking powder
- 1/5 tsp salt
- 2/3 C (160 g) plain yogurt
- 1 egg yolk
- 1 Tbsp milk
- Flour, for dusting

Milk, as needed
1/3 Tbsp grated Parmesan cheese
Beaten egg, for basting
1 Tbsp granulated sugar

Instructions

1 Drain plain yogurt overnight, then wrap in fresh paper towels and press (see page 74). You should end up with appx. 1/5 C (55 g).

2 In a bowl, sift together flour, potato starch, baking powder and salt, and stir. Add drained yogurt and mix with chopping motions with a plastic card or spatula. Stir in blended egg yolk and milk. Place dough in a plastic bag and set aside for 10 minutes.

3 Sprinkle flour on a board or flat surface and roll out dough. Fold into thirds, flip over and roll again. Fold into thirds again and return to plastic bag for 10 more minutes.

4 Remove from bag and roll out dough again. Spread into a 4 3/4" x 10" rectangle. Baste with milk and sprinkle parmesan cheese on top. Fold edges of dough (narrow sides) in towards middle twice, then fold in half to create a heart shape.

5 Cut folded dough into 3/10" (8 mm) wide pieces and place on parchment-lined tray. Baste heart-shaped cookies with egg and sprinkle with granulated sugar. Bake at 350°F (180°C) for 10 minutes.

Regular heart palmier (3 cookies) 204 calories **Low-cal recipe** 106 calories

Mille-feuille
A low-calorie crust and sweet custard filling

A miracle in sweet and healthy treats. Meltingly sweet custard and fresh fruit combined with a lightweight crust. I only use one egg yolk so it's low in cholesterol as well!

Ingredients
(yields one 4″ x 8″ mille-feuille)

Pie Crust
- 1/2 C + 1 Tbsp (80 g) cake flour (low gluten)
- 1 1/2 Tbsp potato (or corn) starch
- 1/3 tsp baking powder
- 1/5 tsp salt
- 2/3 C (160 g) plain yogurt
- 1 egg yolk
- 1 Tbsp milk
- 1 heaping Tbsp grated Parmesan cheese
- Flour, for dusting
- Beaten egg, for basting

Custard crème filling: see page 15
10 strawberries
Appx. 1/2 C honeydew melon (3 1/2 oz (100 g))
Confectioner's sugar, as needed

Instructions

1 Drain plain yogurt overnight, then wrap in fresh paper towels and press (see page 74). You should end up with about 1/5 C (55 g).

2 In a bowl, sift together flour, potato starch, baking powder and salt, then stir. Add drained yogurt and mix with chopping motions with a plastic card or spatula. Add blended egg yolk and milk and stir. Place dough in a plastic bag and set aside for 10 minutes.

3 Sprinkle flour on board or flat surface and roll out dough into a rectangle. Sprinkle with Parmesan cheese, fold into thirds, flip over and roll out again. Fold into thirds and place again in a plastic bag for 10 minutes.

4 Remove from bag and roll out into a 8"x 12" rectangle. Cut into thirds widthwise. Place on parchment-lined tray and poke holes in dough using a fork. Baste with egg and bake at 350°F (180°C) for 18 minutes. Remove and let cool on a wire rack.

5 Thinly slice the strawberries and melon. Make custard crème (see page 15).

6 Spread custard and fruit evenly between 3 pieces of crust. Garnish with confectioner's sugar and cut into 6 pieces.

Regular mille-feuille (1/6 piece) 282 calories **Low-cal recipe** 172 calories

Dreamy Sweets

A collection of healthy yet stylish and fancy sweets that wouldn't look out of place in a bakery window.

Pumpkin Cheesecake Soufflé
Use yogurt for a low-cal soufflé

The color of pumpkin alone makes it a great choice for cheesecake. Whisk quickly so the meringue stays light and fluffy.

Ingredients
(yields eight 3″ soufflés)

- 2 egg whites
  3 2/3 Tbsp (45 g) sugar
- 2 egg yolks
  3 2/3 Tbsp (45 g) sugar
- 4/5 C (200 g) plain yogurt
- 2/5 C (100 g) boiled *kabocha* pumpkin, mashed
- 2 Tbsp each condensed milk, whole milk
- 4 2/3 Tbsp sifted cake flour (low gluten)
- Dash each cinnamon, vanilla extract

Instructions

1 Drain plain yogurt overnight (see page 74). You should end up with about 2/5 C (100 g) after draining.

2 In a bowl, add egg whites and whisk with a hand mixer. Add sugar gradually and continue to whisk until very stiff peaks form.

3 In a separate bowl, combine egg yolks and sugar, then whisk using a hand mixer. Add yogurt and pumpkin, then blend on low speed.

4 Add both milks and flour, and blend on low speed.

5 Using a rubber spatula, gradually stir in egg whites meringue. Add cinnamon and vanilla extract, and stir.

6 Pour batter into oven-safe soufflé cups. Place cups in a baking pan filled halfway with hot water. Bake at 340°F (170°C) for 18 minutes.

Regular pumpkin soufflé 180 calories ➡ **Low-cal recipe** 116 calories

New York-style Cheesecake
You don't need cream cheese to get that decadent flavor

A staple in any dessert collection, this is a New York-style cheesecake made without any fatty cream cheese. A creamy cake you can't mess up— just add it all to a food processor and you're finished with the hard part.

Ingredients
(yields one 7″ cake)

Pie Crust
- 3 1/4 C (80 g) corn flakes
- 1/2 egg
- 2 Tbsp sugar
- 2 1/2 Tbsp milk

2 1/2 C (600 g) plain yogurt
2/5 C (80 g) sugar
3 1/2 Tbsp (30 g) cake flour, sifted
1/5 C (50 ml) milk
2 1/2 eggs
1 1/2 Tbsp lemon juice
Dash vanilla extract
Mint leaves

Instructions

1 Drain plain yogurt overnight (see page 74). You should end up with about 1 1/5 C (300 g).

2 Add all crust ingredients to a plastic bag and mix thoroughly. Set aside for 10 minutes.

3 Take a 10" piece of parchment paper and wet one side, then wipe dry. Place crust on top of paper, then place plastic wrap on top of crust. Press crust into a 7" circle. Place paper, crust and plastic wrap into 7" round baking pan. Push crust firmly into pan, then remove plastic wrap.

4 In a food processor, add drained yogurt, sugar and flour, and blend for 10 seconds. Add milk, lightly beaten egg, lemon juice and vanilla extract. Mix for 10 seconds or until smooth.

5 Pour cake mixture over crust. Bake in oven at 340°F (170°C) for 25 minutes. Remove and garnish with mint leaves.

Regular cheesecake (1/8 slice) 241 calories ➡ **Low-cal recipe** 169 calories

Rare Cheesecake
It's impossible to mess up this sweet cake

The drained yogurt is key to making this creamy cheesecake.
In Egypt and Turkey, drained yogurt is eaten like cheese.

Ingredients
(yields one 7" pie)

2 C (500 g) plain yogurt
1/3 C (70 g) sugar
2/3 C (150 ml) milk
⌐ 1/3 oz (9 g) powder gelatin
└ 3 Tbsp water
1/2 lemon
Dash Grand Marnier
Dash vanilla extract

Blueberry Sauce
⌐ 1 C (140 g) blueberries
   (fresh or frozen)
 2 Tbsp sugar
└ Juice of 1/2 lemon

Instructions

1 Drain plain yogurt overnight (see page 74). You should end up with about 1 C (250 g) after draining. Combine water and gelatin.

2 In a bowl, stir together yogurt and sugar.

3 In a small pot, warm milk. When steam rises, remove from heat and add gelatin. When cooled, add to bowl with yogurt and sugar. Zest lemon peel and add to pot. Squeeze juice from lemon into pot and stir. Add Grand Marnier and vanilla extract.

4 Rinse baking pan with water, then add batter. Place in refrigerator until firm.

5 If using frozen blueberries, allow to thaw. Add blueberries and sugar to a microwave-safe bowl and lightly mash. Add lemon juice, cover with plastic wrap and heat for 4 minutes. Let cool and then garnish cake with blueberry sauce.

Regular cheesecake (1/6 slice) 279 calories **Low-cal recipe** 146 calories

Tiramisu

No need to worry about calories

I developed this low-cal version because so many students asked for it. You'll be so surprised by the rich chocolate taste you won't even miss the calorie-laden mascarpone cheese.

Ingredients

(yields one 6″ square cake)

Sponge Cake

- 2 eggs
- 4 Tbsp (50 g) sugar
- 3 1/2 Tbsp (30 g) cake flour (low gluten)
- 3 3/4 Tbsp (20 g) cocoa
- 1 Tbsp milk

Tiramisu Crème

- 1 2/3 C (400 g) plain yogurt
- 1 egg yolk
- 4 Tbsp (50 g) sugar
- 1 Tbsp cake flour
- 1/3 C (90 ml) milk

Syrup

- 2 Tbsp (25 g) sugar
- 2/5 C hot water
- 1 1/2 tsp instant coffee
- Dash brandy
- 1 Tbsp cocoa

Instructions

1 Drain plain yogurt overnight (see page 74). You should end up with appx. 4/5 C (200 g). Line a baking pan with parchment paper.

2 Make the cake: in a bowl, add eggs and sugar, and whisk with hand mixer until thickened. Sift together flour and cocoa, add milk and stir thoroughly. Pour batter into lined pan and bake in oven for 18 minutes at 340°F (170°C). Let cool on wire rack.

3 Next make the crème: in a bowl, add egg yolk, sugar, flour and a small amount of milk. Whisk until pale yellow. Whisk in remaining milk.

4 Strain crème into a pot and bring to a boil over medium heat. Remove from heat and mix in yogurt. Pour into a container and refrigerate.

5 In a bowl, combine syrup ingredients. Cut the sponge cake in half widthwise (creating 2 thin cakes) and place bottom half in parchment-lined pan. Coat with half the syrup.

6 Cover cake with half the tiramisu crème and layer second half of cake on top. Coat top cake with syrup, then cover with remaining crème. Dust with cocoa.

Regular tiramisu (1/9 slice) 186 calories ➡ **Low-cal recipe** 121 calories

Chocolate Brownies
A low-calorie, highly satisfying chocolate brownie recipe

Take the cocoa butter out of chocolate and you end up with plain cocoa. Plain cocoa has fewer calories than flour! Mix cocoa, syrup and condensed milk and you've got a great chocolate base for your brownies.

Ingredients
(makes one 8″ square)

A
- 1/3 C (30 g) cocoa
- 3 Tbsp (60 g) starch syrup
- 3 Tbsp + 1/2 tsp (60 g) condensed milk

- 2 egg whites
- 2 4/5 Tbsp (35 g) sugar

- 2 egg yolks
- 2 4/5 Tbsp (35 g) sugar

- 1/3 C (50 g) cake flour (low gluten)
- 2 Tbsp (10 g) cocoa

1/5 C (50 ml) milk
2 Tbsp (15 g) walnuts
Confectioner's sugar, as needed

Instructions

1 Sift together flour and cocoa. Spread walnuts on a baking sheet and heat in oven for 10 minutes at 340°F (170°C). Crumble by hand into small pieces.

2 In a small pot, combine mixture A. Add water to a large pot and heat. Place small pot with chocolate mixture into heated water and stir constantly. Line a baking pan with parchment paper.

3 Add egg whites to a bowl and gradually add sugar while whisking with a hand mixer. Whisk until stiff peaks form.

4 In a separate bowl, add egg yolks and sugar and whisk until pale yellow. Gradually mix in egg white meringue with a rubber spatula. Add cocoa mixture into bowl and mix.

5 Add sifted flour, walnuts and milk, then stir. Pour into pan and cook at 350°F (180°C) for 17 minutes.

6 Cool on wire rack and garnish with confectioner's sugar.

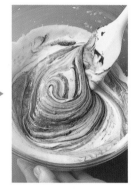

Regular brownie (1/9 piece) 220 calories ➡ **Low-cal recipe** 134 calories

Apricot Square Cake
Butter cake sans butter

The baked apricots give the cake the perfect mix of sweet and tart. I use syrup and condensed milk instead of fattening butter. Cooking in the kitchen has never been so much fun. Be sure to try some while it's warm.

Ingredients
(yields one 8″ square cake)

16 apricots (canned), halved
⌈ 1 C (130 g) cake flour (low gluten)
⌊ 1 Tbsp almond powder
2 eggs
1/3 C (65 g) sugar
⌈ 2 Tbsp (40 g) starch syrup
| 1 Tbsp milk
⌊ 2 Tbsp condensed milk
1 Tbsp Kirschwasser (German cherry brandy)
Dash vanilla extract
2 Tbsp granulated sugar
Apricot jam, as needed

Instructions

1 Line a baking sheet with parchment paper and bake almond powder at 340°F (170°C) for 10 minutes to toast. Sift together toasted almond powder and flour.

2 In a microwave-safe bowl, add starch syrup and milk and heat for 20 seconds. Add condensed milk and stir.

3 In a bowl, combine eggs and sugar and whisk with a hand mixer until thickened. Add syrup mixture from step 2 using a rubber spatula.

4 Add sifted flour and mix briefly. Stir in Kirschwasser and vanilla extract.

5 Pour batter into pan and bake at 350°F (180°C) for 13 minutes. Remove from oven and evenly place apricot halves on top. Sprinkle with granulated sugar.

6 Bake for another 15 minutes. Remove and coat with apricot jam.

Regular apricot cake (1/8 piece) 276 calories ➔ **Low-cal recipe** 195 calories

Chesnut and Brandy Cake
A sweet nip for a midday treat

This cake is an adult favorite with brandy mixed in. If chestnuts are in season, buy some and sweeten them yourself for a totally home-made dessert.

Ingredients
(yields one 9" x 3 1/2" x 2 3/5" cake)

6 candied (sweet boiled) chestnuts
⌐ 2/3 C (90 g) cake flour (low gluten)
└ 1 Tbsp almond powder
2 eggs
2/5 C (90 g) sugar
2 Tbsp (40 g) starch syrup
1 Tbsp milk
2 1/2 Tbsp (40 ml) brandy
Dash vanilla extract
⌐ 1/3 C (80 ml) brandy
A │ 2 1/2 Tbsp (50 g) starch syrup
└ 2 Tbsp each sugar, water

Instructions

1 Bake almond powder at 340°F (170°C) for 10 minutes to toast. Sift together toasted almond powder and flour.

2 In a microwave-safe bowl, combine starch syrup and milk, and heat for 10 to 20 seconds.

3 Slice 2 chestnuts in half and set aside (for use as garnish). Dice remaining chestnuts into 1/5" cubes. Line a baking pan with parchment paper.

4 In a bowl, combine eggs and sugar, then whisk with a hand mixer until thickened. Add syrup mixture and blend.

5 Stir in sifted flour with a rubber spatula. Stir in diced chestnuts, brandy and vanilla extract.

6 Pour batter into pan and bake at 350°F (180°C) for 20 minutes.

7 In a microwave-safe bowl, add starch syrup, sugar, and water from mixture A and heat for 10 to 20 seconds. Stir in brandy.

8 While the cake is cooling, coat with mixture A and garnish with halved chestnuts.

Regular chestnut cake (1/9 piece) **337** calories ➡ Low-cal recipe **161** calories

Baumkuchen
A healthy take on a household favorite

This dessert is usually made with a large amount of butter and baked on a specially-made machine. This homemade version relies on teflon pans instead.
Spread the batter thinly and make a light, fluffy, stacked cake.

Ingredients
(yields one 4" x 5" x 2" cake)

- 2/3 C (95 g) cake flour (low gluten)
- 2 Tbsp (20 g) almond powder
- 3 eggs
- 1/2 C (100 g) sugar
- 2 Tbsp milk
- 1 Tbsp starch syrup
- 2 Tbsp condensed milk
- Dash rum
- Dash vanilla extract
- A ⌈ 2 2/3 Tbsp sugar
  ⌊ 1/3 Tbsp egg

Instructions

1. Bake almond powder at 340°F (170°C) for 10 minutes to toast. Sift toasted almond powder and flour together.

2. In a microwave-safe bowl, combine starch syrup and milk and heat for 10 to 20 seconds. Stir in condensed milk.

3. In a bowl, combine eggs and sugar, and whisk with a hand mixer until thickened. Add syrup mixture and rum, and mix again.

4. Stir in sifted flour with a rubber spatula. Stir in vanilla extract.

5. Use a small, rectangular frying pan (or omelet pan), and heat on medium. Pour a ladleful of batter into pan and spread into a thin layer. When the thin cake is cooked, add 1/3 ladleful of batter on top and flip over. Repeat with remaining batter.

6. Combine mixture A. While cake is still warm, coat with icing. Slice off uneven edges.

Regular Baumkuchen (1/8 piece) 275 calories ➡ **Low-cal recipe** 157 calories

Almond and Pear Tart
Naturally sweet!

This low-calorie tart recipe comes packed with an almond goodness that took three years to perfect. The yogurt provides a creamy filling and you can always switch up the fruits for a new flavor.

Ingredients
(yields one 7" tart)

Tart Crust
- 2 Tbsp (30 g) egg
- 1/5 C (40 g) sugar
- 3/4 C (100 g) cake flour (low gluten)
- 1 Tbsp + 1 tsp (20ml) milk
- Dash vanilla extract
- Cake flour, for dusting

Filling
- 7 1/2 oz (220 g) canned pears (in water)
- 1/3 C (80 g) plain yogurt
- 1/5 C (40 g) sugar
- 1 egg
- 1 Tbsp milk
- 2 Tbsp (20 g) almond powder
- 1 Tbsp (10 g) cake flour
- Dash vanilla extract
- 8 sliced almonds

Instructions

1 Drain plain yogurt overnight (see page 74). You should end up with about 2 1/2 Tbsp (40 g).

2 Thinly slice pears. Dust pan with plenty of flour.

3 Make crust: in a bowl, combine egg and sugar, and whisk. Add flour and vanilla extract and mix with chopping motions with a plastic card or spatula. Stir in milk gradually, checking for proper consistency. Move to a board or flat surface and gently knead. Place in a plastic bag and set aside for 10 minutes.

4 Dust work surface with flour and use a rolling pin to roll dough into 8" circle. Press into pie pan. Roll pin across top to slice off excess dough. Poke holes in bottom using a fork.

5 Make filling: in a bowl, combine yogurt and sugar and mix with a rubber spatula. Add egg, milk, almond powder, flour and vanilla extract, and stir.

6 Pour filling into pie pan. Arrange sliced pears and almonds on top. Cook at 350°F (180°C) for 25 minutes.

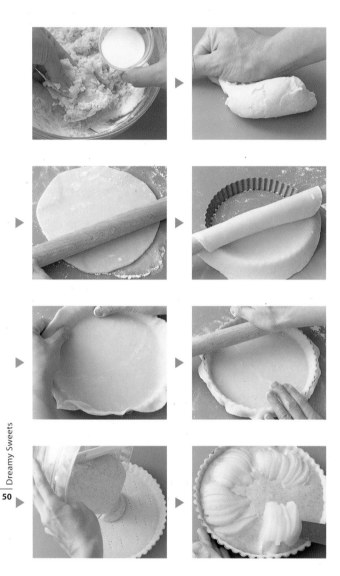

Regular tart (1/6 piece) 266 calories ➡ **Low-cal recipe** 184 calories

Chocolate Tart
The magic of cocoa

A creamy chocolate tart, but no one will notice that it's made without baking chocolate. Make three small tarts or one big 7" tart. Either way, it's all sweet with very little fat.

Ingredients
(yields three 4" tarts)

Tart Crust
Refer to page 50

Filling
- 1 egg
- 2/5 C (80 g) sugar
- 2/3 C (60 g) cocoa
- 3 Tbsp (60 g) condensed milk
- 1 1/2 Tbsp (30 g) starch syrup
- 2/5 C (110 ml) milk

Instructions

1 In a microwave-safe bowl, combine condensed milk and starch syrup, then heat for 10 to 20 seconds.

2 Warm milk to room temperature. Dust pan with flour.

3 Follow instructions on page 50 and make crust. Instead of making one large crust, separate dough into three equal parts, then roll each into circles 6" in diameter. Press into 4" pie pans. Poke holes in bottom with a fork.

4 Make the filling: in a bowl, combine egg and sugar and whisk well. Stir in cocoa and syrup mixture. Mix in milk gradually.

5 Pour filling into pans. Bake for 25 minutes at 340°F (170°C). If making one large tart, bake for 35 minutes.

Regular tart (1/3 piece) 387 calories **Low-cal recipe** 168 calories

Cheese and Pineapple Tart
Made with smooth, creamy yogurt

Pineapple and cheese are perfect companions.
The filling isn't thick at first, but it's fantastic once you bake it.

Ingredients
(yields one 7" tart pan (nonstick))

Tart Crust
Refer to page 50

Filling
- 2 rings pineapple (canned or fresh)
- 4/5 C (200 g) plain yogurt
- 1 egg
- 2 2/5 Tbsp (30 g) sugar
- 1 2/3 Tbsp cake flour (low gluten)
- 2 Tbsp (40 g) condensed milk
- 2/5 C pineapple juice
- 3 Tbsp lemon juice
- Dash vanilla extract

Instructions

1 Drain plain yogurt overnight (see page 74). You should end up with appx. 2/5 C (100 g).

2 Follow instructions on page 50 and make crust. Dust the pie pan with plenty of flour and press dough into pan.

3 Make the filling: in a bowl, combine yogurt, egg, and sugar and whisk thoroughly. Mix in flour. Stir in milk, both juices and vanilla extract.

4 Pour filling into pie pan and bake at 320°F (160°C) for 10 minutes. Remove from oven and add chopped pineapples to tart. Place back in oven and bake for 25 minutes more.

Regular tart (1/6 piece) 292 calories Low-cal recipe 196 calories

Handmade Truffles
No self-restraint necessary with these chocolates!

Don't you want chocolate without the guilt?
I'll show you how to make these decadent treats.
If you use good quality cocoa, you'll be fully satisfied
the moment it melts in your mouth. It makes a sweet
present too!

Ingredients
(yields 10 truffles)

4/5 C (70 g) cocoa
1/2 C (100 g) sugar
1/4 C (70 ml) milk
⌐ 1 1/4 tsp (3 g) powder gelatin
└ 1 1/2 Tbsp water
1 Tbsp rum
⌐ 20 raisins (10 g)
└ 2 tsp rum
Cocoa, for coating

Instructions

1 In a microwave-safe bowl, combine gelatin powder and water.

2 Soak raisins in rum.

3 In a separate bowl, combine cocoa and sugar. Stir in milk gradually.

4 Microwave the soaked gelatin for 5 to 10 seconds, then add to cocoa mixture. Stir in rum. Chill mixture in refrigerator.

5 Scoop up a clump of chilled chocolate with a spoon and add a few raisins to the center. With a second spoon, form a small, round truffle.

6 Add truffle to dry cocoa powder and coat lightly.

Regular truffles (2 per serving) 210 calories ➡ **Low-cal recipe** 148 calories

Sachertorte
A high-fat cake transformed into a low-cal wonder

This is the perfect cocoa-based treat.
With a rich chocolate coating, you'd never guess that this is actually low-fat. It's also a perfect Valentine's day gift for your loved one.

Ingredients
(yields one 7" heart-shaped cake)

2/3 C (100 g) cake flour (low gluten)
1/2 C (40 g) cocoa
- 2 egg yolks
- 3 2/3 Tbsp (45 g) sugar
- 2 egg whites
- 3 2/3 Tbsp (45 g) sugar
- 3 Tbsp (60 g) starch syrup
- 1/3 C (70 ml) milk
- 1 1/4 Tbsp (20 ml) rum

A
- 1/4 Tbsp (5 g) starch syrup
- 3 Tbsp milk
- 1/4 C (50 g) sugar
- 1/3 C (30 g) cocoa

2 slices roasted almond

Instructions

1 Sift together flour and cocoa.

2 In a microwave-safe bowl, combine starch syrup and milk, and heat for 20 seconds. Stir in rum.

3 In a bowl, add egg whites and whisk with a hand mixer while gradually adding sugar until very stiff peaks form.

4 In a separate bowl, combine egg yolks and sugar. Whisk with a hand mixer until pale yellow. Stir in syrup mixture, then cocoa mixture. Gradually add egg white meringue.

5 Line heart-shaped pan with parchment paper and pour in batter. Bake at 350°F (180°C) for 30 minutes.

6 In a small pot, add syrup and milk from mixture A and heat. When blended, add sugar and cocoa and stir until smooth.

7 When cake is done, remove from oven. Spread chocolate frosting on cake while still warm. Garnish with almond slices.

Regular sachertorte (1/10 piece) 256 calories ➡ **Low-cal recipe** 156 calories

Coffee Soufflé Roll
A soft and gentle taste that's nice to your body too!

This is a light and fluffy sponge cake rolled with a cool coffee flavored custard filling.
The light sweetness swirled with the bitter coffee is definitely a grown-up flavor.

Ingredients (yields one 12" roll)

Sponge Cake
- 2 egg whites
- 3 2/3 Tbsp (45 g) sugar
- 2 egg yolks
- 1 tsp instant coffee
- 2 tsp hot water
- 2 2/3 Tbsp (40 ml) milk
- 4 2/3 Tbsp bread flour
  (high gluten), sifted
- 1 Tbsp diced almonds

Coffee Custard
- 1 egg yolk
- 2 Tbsp cake flour
  (low gluten)
- 4 Tbsp (50 g) sugar
- 2 tsp instant coffee
- 4/5 C (200 ml) milk
- Dash vanilla extract

Instructions

1 Make custard first: in a bowl, add egg yolk, flour, sugar, instant coffee, and a small amount of milk, then whisk well. Stir in remaining milk, then pour contents through a strainer and into a saucepan. Stir with rubber spatula over medium heat until mixture boils. Remove from heat and stir in vanilla extract. Pour into bowl, cover with plastic wrap and let cool.

2 Make sponge cake: in a bowl, add egg whites and whisk with a hand mixer. Add sugar gradually and whisk until stiff peaks form.

3 In a small bowl, add instant coffee and hot water and stir. Stir in milk.

4 In another bowl, add egg yolks and coffee mixture from step 3, then blend on low speed using a hand mixer. Gradually add in the egg white meringue while stirring quickly with a rubber spatula. Add the bread flour and stir briefly.

5 Line a 10" x 12" baking pan with parchment paper. Add cake batter evenly, then sprinkle with diced almonds. Cook at 350°F (180°C) for 10 minutes.

6 Remove from oven, cover with another pan to trap steam and let cool.

7 Remove sponge cake from baking pan and transfer to a clean sheet of paper. To make rolling the sponge easier, make 3 shallow incisions 1/3" (1 cm) apart from one edge. Make a diagonal slice at the opposite edge of the cake. Spread custard over cake then gently roll the cake starting with scored edge.

Regular coffee roll (1/8 piece) 210 calories ➡ **Low-cal recipe** 124 calories

Bouche de Noel
A simple treat for a special occasion

Bouche de Noel, or Yule Log, is a traditional Christmas cake. The yogurt-base cream cheese holds the cake together while the light whipping cream gives the icing a fragrant sweetness. This is my favorite "special occasion" cake.

Ingredients
(yields one 12″ roll)

Sponge Cake
- 2 eggs
- 1/5 C (40 g) sugar
- 4 2/3 Tbsp (40 g) cake flour, sifted
- 1 Tbsp milk

Cream Cheese Filling
- 1 2/3 C (400 g) plain yogurt
- 4 Tbsp (50 g) sugar
- 2/5 C (110 ml) milk

Icing
- 2/5 C (80 g) sugar
- 2 Tbsp light whipping cream (30% fat)

15 fresh raspberries
3 to 4 mint leaves

Instructions

1 Drain plain yogurt overnight (see page 74). You should end up with appx. 4/5 C (200 g).

2 Make sponge cake: in a bowl, whisk eggs and sugar with a hand mixer until thickened.

3 Mix in flour with a rubber spatula. Stir in milk.

4 Line a 10" x 12" pan with parchment paper. Add batter evenly, and bake at 350°F (180°C) for 9 minutes.

5 Remove from oven, cover with another pan and let cool.

6 In a bowl, combine cream cheese filling ingredients and stir. In another bowl, combine icing ingredients.

7 Remove sponge cake from paper liner and lay over a clean piece of paper. To make rolling the cake easier, make 3 shallow incisions 1/2" apart from one edge. Make a diagonal slice at the opposite edge of the cake.

8 Mince 10 raspberries and set remaining 5 aside for use as garnish. Spread cream cheese filling onto cake, then sprinkle minced raspberries on top. Gently roll cake, starting with scored edge.

9 Spread icing onto cake and garnish with raspberries and mint leaves.

Regular bouche de Noel (1/8 piece) **200** calories ➤ **Low-cal recipe** **158** calories

Cool Confections

After dinner or when you want something sweet, healthy as can be, these are the perfect cool treats for a hot summer day.

Custard Bavarois
Make it without heavy cream

Regular bavarois is made with cream, which makes it surprisingly high-calorie. I use egg white meringue to get a lightweight, low-cal version. Garnish with fresh fruits that are in season for an extra helping of sweetness.

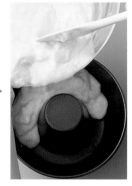

Ingredients
(yields one 7″ ring)

1 C (250 g) plain yogurt
⌐ 2 egg yolks
∟ 2/5 C (80 g) sugar
1 C (250 ml) milk
⌐ 2 1/3 Tbsp powder gelatin
∟ 1/3 C (90 ml) water
⌐ 2 egg whites
∟ 1 1/5 Tbsp sugar
Dash vanilla extract
Dash Grand Marnier

Yogurt Sauce
⌐ 4/5 C (200 g) plain yogurt
│ 2 2/5 Tbsp (30 g) sugar
∟ 1 Tbsp Grand Marnier
1/2 grapefruit
1/4 orange

Instructions

1 Combine gelatin and water.

2 Combine egg yolks and sugar in a bowl and whisk until pale yellow. Add milk, then pour into a heated pan. Cook until mixture bubbles, then turn off heat. Add gelatin and stir until fully dissolved.

3 In another bowl, add yogurt and contents of the pan. Place bowl on top of a separate bowl filled with ice water to chill while stirring. Stir constantly until mixture is creamy.

4 In a separate bowl, add egg whites and gradually whisk in sugar with a hand mixer. Continue to whisk until soft peaks form.

5 Add meringue to chilled mixture from step 3 and stir quickly. Stir in vanilla extract and Grand Marnier. Rinse a bavarois mold with water, then add mixture and place in refrigerator to harden.

6 Combine yogurt sauce ingredients in a bowl and whisk.

7 Peel grapefruit and orange and slice.

8 Serve bavarois on a plate, place fruit in center and garnish with yogurt sauce.

Regular bavarois (1/8 piece) 302 calories ➜ **Low-cal recipe** 148 calories

Peach Bavarois
Have fun with fruit variations

I added peach purée to the bavarois mix for a fruity twist. You can use fresh peaches, too. Try pears, strawberries or even bananas!

Ingredients (serves 6)

10 oz (280 g) white peaches (canned)
2/3 C (150 g) plain yogurt
1 egg yolk
1/3 C (60 g) sugar
2/3 C (150 ml) milk
2 Tbsp (14 g) powder gelatin
1/4 C (60 ml) water
2 Tbsp lemon juice
1/2 Tbsp Grand Marnier
1 egg white
1 1/5 Tbsp (15 g) sugar
1/5 C (50 g) white peaches (canned)
Mint leaves, for garnish

Instructions

1 Combine gelatin and water. Add yogurt and peaches to a mixer and purée until smooth. Transfer to a bowl.

2 In a separate bowl, combine egg yolk and sugar, and whisk while gradually adding a small amount of milk. Stir in remaining milk, then pour into heated pan and simmer. Once mixture bubbles, remove from heat and add gelatin. Stir until gelatin is fully dissolved.

3 Add mixture from step 2 and lemon juice to mixture from step 1. Stir in Grand Marnier. Place bowl on top of a bowl filled with ice water to chill while stirring. Stir constantly until mixture is creamy.

4 In a separate bowl, add egg whites and gradually whisk in sugar with a hand mixer. Continue to whisk until soft peaks form.

5 Add meringue to chilled mixture from step 3 and stir quickly with a rubber spatula. Pour into container and place in refrigerator overnight to harden. Garnish with sliced white peaches and mint leaves before serving.

Regular bavarois 255 calories **Low-cal recipe** 144 calories

Raspberry Mousse
A fluffy meringue that's very low in calories

Fresh pink mousse with an ample dose of raspberries.
The sweet and sour combo of fruit and yogurt melts in your mouth.
Of course, making this with strawberries is delicious, too!

Ingredients
(yields six 4″ cup servings)

A ⎡ 5 1/4 oz (150 g) raspberries
  ⎢   (fresh or frozen)
  ⎢ 1 C (250 g) plain yogurt
  ⎣ 2/5 C (80 g) sugar
⎡ 2 Tbsp (15 g) powder gelatin
⎣ 2/5 C (100 ml) water
⎡ 1 egg white
⎣ 2 1/2 Tbsp (30 g) sugar
1 to 2 raspberries, for garnishing

Instructions

1 In a microwave-safe bowl, combine gelatin
and water. Microwave for 5 to 10 seconds to
dissolve.

2 Add mixture A to a blender and blend until
smooth. Transfer to a bowl, and stir in gelatin. Place bowl in another bowl filled with ice
water and stir until mixture thickens.

3 In a bowl, add egg whites and gradually whisk
in sugar with a hand mixer until soft peaks
form. Add to chilled mixture from step 2 and
stir lightly.

4 Pour mousse into 4" soufflé cups and place in
refrigerator to harden. Thinly slice raspberries
and place on top before serving.

Regular mousse 241 calories ➡ **Low-cal recipe** 117 calories

Pudding
Even without the high-calorie cream, it's creamy and smooth

When soft, melt-in-your-mouth pudding was the craze, I wanted to try making it myself but discovered all the recipes called for a lot of cream. Here, instead of cream I used gelatin and milk to get that same super-soft pudding.

Ingredients
(serves 6)

2 eggs
1 2/3 C (400 ml) milk
1/3 C (65 g) sugar
⌐ 1 1/4 tsp (3 g) powder gelatin
∟ 1 Tbsp water
Dash vanilla extract

Caramel Sauce
⌐ 4 Tbsp (50 g) sugar
│ 2 Tbsp water
∟ 1 Tbsp hot water

Instructions

1 Make caramel sauce: in a small pan, combine sugar and water. Cook over medium heat until sugar turns dark brown. Remove from heat and add hot water. Rock the pan back and forth to even out the color. Quickly pour into pudding cups.

2 Make pudding: combine gelatin and water. Add milk and sugar to a pot and heat over medium until sugar dissolves. Remove from heat and add gelatin. Stir until completely dissolved.

3 Add eggs to a bowl and whisk thoroughly.

4 After mixture from step 2 has cooled, gradually stir into whisked eggs. Stir in vanilla extract gently. Try not to add any bubbles.

5 Pour mixture into cups with caramel sauce. Skim any froth.

6 Fill a baking pan halfway with hot water. Place cups in pan and cook in oven for 45 minutes at 300°F (150°C). Remove, let cool, then chill in refrigerator.

Regular pudding 194 calories ➡ **Low-cal recipe** 142 calories

Chocolate Soufflé
Even without baking chocolate, this soufflé has a rich flavor

On the outside, soufflé. On the inside, melted chocolate. This is a mysterious confection. It seems like a lot of work but it's really quite simple. Enjoy it warm or chilled.

Ingredients
(yields one 5" soufflé)

- 1 egg white
- 2 1/2 tsp (10 g) sugar
- 1 egg yolk
- 2 2/5 Tbsp (30 g) sugar
- 1 Tbsp starch syrup
- 3 3/4 Tbsp (20 g) cocoa
- 2 tsp (6 g) cake flour (low gluten)
- 1/2 C (130 ml) milk
- 1 Tbsp rum
- Dash vanilla extract

Instructions

1 Sift together flour and cocoa. Pour starch syrup into a microwave-safe bowl and heat for 10 seconds.

2 Add egg whites to a bowl and gradually whisk in sugar with a hand mixer. Whisk until stiff peaks form.

3 In a separate bowl, add egg yolk and sugar and mix on low speed with a hand mixer until even. Add heated syrup, and mix. Add cocoa mixture and syrup and whisk on low speed. Gradually blend in milk, then add rum and vanilla extract.

4 Gradually stir in egg white meringue. Pour batter into a soufflé cup. Fill a baking pan halfway with hot water. Place cup in pan and cook in oven for 30 minutes at 320°F (160°C). Poke with a skewer. If it comes out clean, remove from oven and let cool. Place in refrigerator to harden.

Regular soufflé (1/8 piece) 201 calories **Low-cal recipe** 119 calories

Milk Pudding
To stimulate your metabolism, use kudzu starch

This is a popular, cheap dessert at convenience stores in Japan. My students requested a healthy version. Agar gives it that unique taste, so be sure to use agar and not a substitute.

Ingredients
(yields six 1/2 C servings)

A
- 2 tsp (5 g) agar powder
- 1/3 C (60 g) sugar
- 1 2/3 C (400 ml) milk
- 2 3/4 Tbsp (22 g) kudzu starch (or arrowroot)
- 2/5 C (100 ml) water
- Dash vanilla extract

B
- 1/2 tsp (2 g) agar powder
- 1/3 C (40 g) unpacked brown sugar
- 2/5 C (100 ml) water

1 Tbsp (5 g) soy flour (*kinako*)

Instructions

1 Mash sugar into agar from mixture A.

2 Mash brown sugar into agar from mixture B.

3 Add milk to a pan and heat over medium heat. Stir in sugar and agar from step 1 gradually. When mixture boils, reduce heat to low and simmer. Add kudzu flour to water and dissolve. Add kudzu mixture to pot and stir thoroughly.

4 Remove from heat and stir in vanilla extract. Pour mixture into cups. After pudding has cooled place in refrigerator to chill.

5 Add water from mixture B to a pot and heat over medium heat. Slowly stir in sugar and agar from step 2. Once the mixture boils, turn heat to low and simmer until mixture is thoroughly liquefied. Remove from heat and let cool. Pour mixture onto pudding in cups, then place in refrigerator to harden. Garnish with a pinch of soy flour on each before serving.

Regular milk pudding 159 calories **Low-cal recipe** 118 calories

Vanilla Ice Cream
A modest amount of egg—and no cream!

Regular ice cream uses a lot of eggs and fresh cream, and is very high in calories.
But this creamy treat uses just a little egg, plus flour and milk.
Give it a good whisk for that smooth texture that melts in your mouth.

Ingredients
(yields six 3 1/2 oz servings)

- 1 egg yolk
- 4 Tbsp (50 g) sugar
- 2 tsp cake flour (low gluten)
- 1 C (250 ml) milk
- 1 tsp (2 g) powder gelatin
- 1 tsp water
- Dash vanilla extract
- 1 egg white
- 1 1/5 Tbsp (15 g) sugar

Instructions

1 Combine gelatin and water.

2 In a bowl, combine egg yolk, sugar and flour and gradually add a little milk while whisking. Whisk in remaining milk.

3 Strain mixture from step 2 into a pot and heat. When steam rises, remove from heat and add gelatin. Mix with a rubber spatula until gelatin is completely dissolved. Stir in vanilla extract.

4 Place pot over a bowl of ice water and stir constantly until mixture thickens.

5 In a bowl, add egg white, and gradually add sugar while whisking with a hand mixer. Whisk until soft peaks form. Add egg white meringue gradually to pot from step 4.

6 Pour mixture into a container and let harden in freezer.

Regular ice cream **140** calories ➡ Low-cal recipe **86** calories

Sweet Potato and Rum Raisin Ice Cream
A healthy ice cream!

Sweet potatoes have vitamin C and minerals which keep your body healthy.
Mixed into ice cream, this veggie turns into a super tasty treat. Rum raisins are the perfect accent.

Ingredients
(Serves 8)

5 1/4 oz (150 g) sweet potato
⌐ 1 egg yolk
| 1/3 C (60 g) sugar
| 1 1/2 tsp (4 g) cake flour (low gluten)
⌐ 1 C (250 ml) milk
⌐ 1 tsp (2 g) powder gelatin
⌐ 1 tsp water
Dash cinnamon
Dash vanilla extract
⌐ 1 egg white
⌐ 1 1/5 Tbsp (15 g) sugar
⌐ 20 raisins (10 g)
⌐ 2 tsp rum
1 Tbsp rum

Instructions

1 Combine gelatin and water. Soak raisins in 2 tsp rum. Peel sweet potato, soak briefly in water, then boil. Press through a strainer. You should end up with appx. 1/5 C (70 g).

2 In a bowl, combine egg yolk, sugar and flour and gradually add a little milk while whisking. Whisk in remaining milk.

3 Add mixture from step 2 to a pan and heat. Once steam rises, remove from heat and add gelatin. Mix until gelatin is completely dissolved. Add strained sweet potato and stir with a spatula. Add cinnamon and vanilla extract, and mix.

4 Place pan over a bowl of ice water and stir constantly until mixture thickens.

5 In a bowl, add egg white, and gradually add sugar while whisking with a hand mixer. Whisk until soft peaks form. Add egg white meringue gradually to pot from step 4. Add rum and rum-soaked raisins and stir. Pour into a container and place in freezer to harden.

Regular ice cream 151 calories **Low-cal recipe** 88 calories

Mango Frozen Yogurt
Our favorite healthy dessert

All you have to do is cut up fruit into bite-size pieces, freeze them,
then whip them into a quick dessert. This is the most popular dessert at my house.

Ingredients
(Serves 4)

5 1/4 oz (150 g) mango
4/5 C (200 g) plain yogurt
1 egg white
2 Tbsp honey
1 Tbsp Grand Marnier

Instructions

1 Cut mangoes into bite-size pieces and place in freezer.

2 Drain plain yogurt overnight (see page 74). You should end up with about 2/5 C (100 g).

3 In a bowl, whisk egg white with a hand mixer until soft peaks form. Add honey and whisk until stiff peaks form.

4 Add drained yogurt, frozen mangoes and Grand Marnier to a blender. Purée until smooth.

5 Add egg white meringue to blender and mix. Pour into a container and let harden in freezer.

Regular frozen yogurt 120 calories ➡ **Low-cal recipe** 91 calories

Basic Techniques

Making Meringue

Egg white meringue is whisked egg whites and sugar. The degree of whisking changes depending on what you're making so take note of the differences.

1 Add egg whites to a bowl and whisk with a hand mixer.

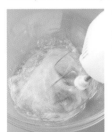
2 Add sugar to the softly beaten whites gradually, adding a third each time.

3 Whisk until the peaks curl down when mixer is lifted. These are soft peaks, used in mousses, etc.

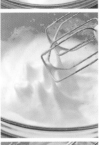
4 Whisk until peaks stand straight up when mixer is lifted. These are stiff peaks, used in cakes, etc.

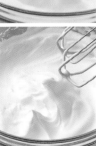
5 Whisk until very stiff peaks form and they hold their shape. These are used for soufflés.

Whisking Eggs

Instead of using butter when making muffins and cakes, I use whole eggs so it's important to whisk them properly. It's important to mix by hand quickly.

1 In a bowl combine eggs and sugar, then whisk with a hand mixer.

2 Whisk gently, allowing the mixture to aerate and turn frothy.

3 Whisk until the mixture is thick and soft peaks form.

4 Using a rubber spatula, mix in milk or other liquid.

5 If using fruit such as bananas, stir into mixture.

6 Add sifted flour and blend in completely.

Drained Yogurt

Drained yogurt is used in place of things like cream cheese, butter and fresh cream. There are two levels, depending on the type of recipe you are making.

1 Spread paper towels in a strainer and add yogurt. Place strainer in a bowl and refrigerate overnight.

2 After draining, the yogurt should have the consistency of fresh cheese and will be half its original weight. If yogurt is still runny, wrap with fresh paper towels. This level can be used for cheesecakes, etc.

3 Remove drained yogurt from strainer and wrap in fresh paper towels. Place a light weight on top and let stand for 1 to 2 hours.

4 It should be thick and dry enough to crumble by hand and will be about a third of its original weight. This can be used in place of butter when making pie crusts, etc.

Custard Crème

With no butter and just a little egg, this is an easy and lightweight crème.

1 In a bowl, combine egg yolk, sugar, cake flour and whisk. Slowly add in just enough milk to combine ingredients.

2 Whisk until thoroughly mixed, then add remaining milk and whisk again.

3 Pour through a strainer into a pot and heat over medium.

4 Mix using a rubber spatula. When mixture bubbles up, remove from heat and stir in vanilla extract.

5 Pour into a pan and cover tightly with plastic wrap. Let cool.

Caramel Sauce

Be sure to rock the pan to keep sauce from burning. For best results, use a non-stick pan.

1 Add sugar and water to pan and heat over medium heat while stirring constantly.

2 When sugar begins to change color, rock pan back and forth until the caramel color evens out.

3 When caramel turns dark brown, remove from heat and slowly add hot water.

4 Rock pan and mix water evenly into caramel.

Using the Oven

Set the oven to the desired temperature and let the oven preheat fully before using. The cooking time will change depending on what kind of oven you have, so always check the baked item with a toothpick or skewer to ensure item is fully cooked. If batter sticks to the skewer, bake for five more minutes. If the skewer comes out clean, remove item from oven and cool on a wire rack. Overbaking will cause items to turn tough, since there's no oil or butter. If it looks done and a skewer comes out cleanly before the cooking time is up, remove from oven early.

Removing a Chiffon Cake

After cake has thoroughly cooled, gently insert a knife around the outside of the cake to loosen it from the tube pan.

1 Insert a knife and carefully saw around the edge to loosen the cake from the side of the pan.

2 Carefully pull cake from the pan.

3 Insert a thin knife against the tube and saw around the edge to loosen the cake from the center.

4 Insert knife underneath cake and carefully run along the edge to loosen cake from the bottom.

5 With one hand on top of cake, flip over. Remove tube and bottom and place on dish.

Making a Cornet

Cornets are used to draw detailed decorations.

1 Cut a 6" x 6" square of parchment paper and cut into 2 triangles.

2 Take one traingle and lay flat. With the widest angle at the top, roll one end toward the inside, matching tips. Roll other end outside, pulling into a cone.

3 Fold tips inside.

4 Add icing, fold over top, and cut off bottom tip.

Baking with quality products

The main ingredients in these cakes are eggs, milk, sugar and flour. Spend a little extra and buy good-quality ingredients. Being able to choose your ingredients is one of the advantages to home-made food. It's important to pick products that you can easily metabolize and won't place an unnecessary burden on your body.

Eggs

When picking eggs, it's essential to consider the environment the chickens were raised in and what their feed was. It's best to choose organic or free-range eggs from chickens that have been raised on vegetable diets such as corn and beans, and from a farm that doesn't use hormones and antibiotics. The color of the shell doesn't matter. The shell's color varies depending on the breed of bird, and the yolk changes color depending on the feed. Freshness is also important. Since there's no fat or grease used, the whisked eggs create an essential lightweight counterpart for cakes. Fresh eggs provide a better meringue. Although egg yolks contain a large amount of cholesterol, none of the recipes call for more than 4 eggs. With 8 servings per dish one person only eats 1/2 an egg. It's important to have a healthy amount, and I've taken care not to use more than necessary.

Milk

Like eggs, the environment for the cattle and their feed are important. Again, antibiotic- and hormone-free cows are best, as well as natural feed. Recently, more supermarkets have been stocking organic milk, so choose organic whenever possible. There's also low-fat milk, but low-fat milks go through an extra process, so try to avoid low-fat if possible. Unprocessed milk has 3.8% fat content. Choose milk that's as close to all-natural as possible.

Wheat Flour

It's best to pick a flour that has not been exposed to agricultural chemicals and fertilizers. Go for organic flour that hasn't been exposed to harmful chemicals.

Sugar

The sugar used in this book is regular white refined sugar. Some people may think that sugar is bad for the body, but it's fine in small amounts. Regular refined white sugar works best.

Products

In Place of Oil and Butter

I use substitutions for butter and oil. Choose organic, high-quality versions of these ingredients as well.

Honey

Honey gives cakes that moist texture and a smooth, rich flavor. If possible, buy organic honey from a natural, chemical-free environment. Avoid any man-made honey substitutes or non-organic versions that might contain antibiotics.

Starch Syrup

Like honey, starch syrup helps cakes retain moisture while baking. You can also use it mixed with cocoa and make a smooth chocolate icing. Corn syrup is naturally sweet and is dark brown in color. I also recommend using syrup derived from glutinous rice.

Condensed Milk

Use condensed millk instead of butter and heavy cream. Condensed milk is 2 to 3 times denser than regular milk and has an 8.3% fat content. Butter is 83% fat! There may not be a wide selection of high quality brands to choose from. Specialty stores will carry a larger selection.

Yogurt

Plain yogurt is drained to make cream cheese and butter substitutes. Yogurt has about the same calorie and fat content as milk. Since cream cheese has 33% fat content, it's far too fatty for these recipes. When you want a cheesy substitute, add a little grated Parmesan to it. Select yogurt in the same way as milk, paying attention to where and how it was manufactured.

Cocoa

Cocoa mixed with condensed milk and syrup is a great substitute for baking chocolate. Cocoa is chocolate minus the cocoa butter. Cocoa butter has a lot of calories and a high fat content, but cocoa powder is low in calories—lower, in fact, than flour. It also provides a great chocolate flavor. I buy organic cocoa powder whenever possible.

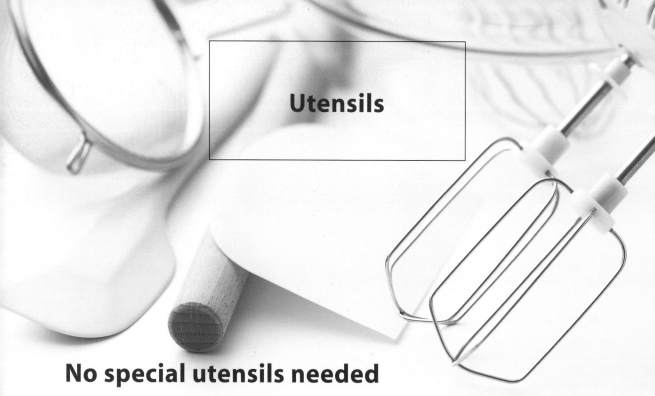

No special utensils needed

Making delicious treats is just as simple as steaming rice. Baking is an easy activity to try out in your kitchen, and you don't even need any special utensils.

Bowls

Use stainless steel bowls, heat-resistant glass bowls, etc. that a hand mixer won't damage or scratch. A deep bowl is best when whisking so the contents won't spill. If you have two large bowls you can make everything with ease.

Hand Mixer

Since whisking the eggs is important in my recipes it's vital to have a hand mixer with variable speed. Kitchenaid and Cuisinart both offer a selection of mixers to choose from and within a reasonable price range, but look for one that has a turbo speed to avoid clogging. Go with a mixer that has stainless steel blades.

Rubber Spatulas

I recommend a heat-safe, seamless spatula for baking. If you use a regular rubber spatula when stirring custard in a heated pot, it can melt, so be sure to use a heat-safe spatula. Different foods can leave residue on rubber spatulas, so I recommend using separate spatulas for baking and for regular cooking.

Sifter

I recommend a sifter with an average gauge that you can work with just one hand. I've tried working with very fine sifters or ones with two layers of mesh, but it took too long to sift the flour. Timing and ease is important in baking, so use utensils that make things easy for you.

Plastic Card

A card has many uses. It can be used to level a sponge cake, to chop dough, or to slow liquids when pouring. It can also be used to clean off the counters afterwards. Using just a cloth is tedious work. Just wet the counter a little and gently scrape off any dough with the card, then rinse with a cloth.

Rolling Pin

Rolling pins are used mainly to rolling dough out when making cookies, tarts and pie crust. Most pins are made of wood, and a 12" pin is probably the easiest size to handle.

Greasing

Since we won't be using any oils or fats even to grease the pans and molds, here's how we make sure everything comes out perfectly.

Paper Baking Cups

These are available in a variety of shapes and sizes. After baking, you can remove the paper easily. They're made from glassine paper. Bread dough will stick, however, so only use this for cakes and muffins.

Oven Paper

If you can't find baking cups in the size or shape desired, cut the shape you need from oven or parchment paper. You can use it in a pan when baking, just be sure to insert it with the right side up.

Using Oven Paper

1 Measure the pan you will use by placing it on top of the paper, then cut.

2 Cut one side at each corner as shown.

3 Fold sides up and tuck into pan.

• When using a circular pan, use two separate pieces for the sides and the bottom.

Baking Sheets

If you bake often it is more economical to buy a non-stick baking sheet (teflon, etc.). After baking, the sheet can be easily rinsed off with water.

Aluminum Foil Pans

When baking tarts or cakes, disposable aluminum pans are very convenient. They come in a variety of shapes and sizes so I recommend trying those as well.

Teflon Materials

It's difficult to find baking cups that work in a tart mold, so using teflon tart molds dusted with flour is the best option. However, be sure to use an aluminum tube pan when cooking chiffon cakes as teflon will prevent it from rising properly. Be sure to use a small knife or metal spatula to loosen the baked good from the teflon pan, otherwise the shape might not hold up properly. Teflon frying pans also eliminate the need for cooking oil.

Kumiko Ibaraki

Ms. Ibaraki is a food scientist. After graduating from St. Luke's College of Nursing, she worked as a public health nurse. She realized then that many modern "lifestyle" illnesses are linked to modern diets. As she was always interested in cooking and baking, she went on to culinary school. She later founded the Ibaraki Cooking Studio, where she teaches students how to make various dishes and baked goods. She has also written articles and books and given lectures on how to make food both healthy and delicious.

THE WORRY-FREE BAKERY

Translation: Jessica Bezer
Vetting: Glory Gallo

Copyright © 2009 by Kumiko Ibaraki
Photography © 2009 by Noriko Aoyama

All rights reserved.

Published by Vertical, Inc., New York.

Originally published in Japanese as *Futoranai Okashi* by Bunka Shuppankyoku, Tokyo, 2005.

ISBN 978-1-934287-69-9

Manufactured in The United States of America

First American Edition

Vertical, Inc.
www.vertical-inc.com